* * * * *

"KABBALAH LESSONS

TO WIN THE GAME OF LIFE"

*

THE CONSCIOUS GAME

DISCOVER KABBALAH EXPLAINED
WITH SOCCER EXAMPLES

LOST ON THE FIELD...

After kicking every ball that came my way without much success, I began to question life. I could not comprehend it, and this filled me with anxiety. I thought that if there was any purpose to it, I had no idea what it was. So, I embarked on buying and reading every book I thought could help me make sense of my life. I was young and naive, just starting my first soccer lessons, yet I already wanted to be a true professional. I undervalued the journey, believing the goal was simply to win, without having played all the matches that lay ahead.

When I was sixteen, my father took me to hear a Kabbalist rabbi who was visiting from Israel. I vividly remember my surprise. It was the first time I'd ever heard of someone who seemed to know what life was about. When I inquired about it, they told me that Kabbalah was forbidden and beyond my understanding. That response was perhaps one of the greatest gifts I could have received because, before they had even finished telling me it was forbidden, I was already looking for ways to dive deeper into it. Back then, it was not easy to study it; everything seemed to conspire against me in my efforts to do so. The *Zohar,* the primary book of Kabbalah, written in Aramaic, was studied only by a few rabbis—there was no place to learn it, nor anyone to teach me. Years later, I heard that a book on Kabbalah had arrived at a nearby bookstore. That's when my relationship with this wisdom began, deeply touching something deep in my heart and telling me this was the path.

I dedicated a lot of time and effort to studying the subject. I joined study groups with people thirty years older than me and listened to recorded lessons on cassettes that came from abroad. That's how I began to learn. Years later, I started reading the Zohar, as by then an English translation had become available. That task took me eight years. I would wake up in the early hours to study, convinced I could shorten the journey and skip a few steps along the way to get to who knows where faster. My only goal was to win.

What worked in my favor was knowing that I wanted to find mentors, not just teachers—a piece of advice my mother always gave me. Life gifted me the opportunity to study Kabbalah alongside her for several years.

Eventually, there came a time when I already knew the basic rules of the game: the passes, the plays, and even some tricks with the ball to impress more than a few. However, within, there was a frustrated player who, no matter how much knowledge he gained, could not seem

It sounds interesting and challenging, doesn't it? Just like when you are about to start a soccer match.

IN THE LOCKER ROOM

In the locker room, players prepare for the challenge that awaits them on the field, as the coach provides final tactics and words of encouragement. Amid lively conversations and gestures of support, the team's unity strengthens, with the thrill of victory pounding in their hearts. In this atmosphere of camaraderie, team bonds strengthen, and each player's spirit ignites fueled by passion for the game and yearning to triumph.

Just as a coach offers guidance before the team takes the field, I would like to share my recommendations to help you make the most of this book.

Keep one thing in mind: don't believe everything that you read here. First, put these ideas into practice in your life and see if they work for you. Similarly, do not believe everything you think. We tend to assume our ideas are true simply because they occurred to us, defending them as if we were bearers of supreme wisdom. It is not about whether the information is true or false but about the mental process involved in assimilating new ideas. Your mind tends to generate an internal dialogue, comparing ideas it already knows (and assumes as truth) with new ones that come to challenge its existing knowledge.

The mind has a need to seek coherence and for its thoughts to make sense, and it is not particularly interested in finding "the truth." For example, when you imagine yourself playing soccer, how do you picture it? You see yourself as a sports star with great skills, don't you? Our thoughts constantly idealize and manipulate our perception, favoring our desires rather than objective reality. A thought is nothing more than a proposal, a suggestion your brain offers you. Instead of thinking, our brains tend to make assumptions, form opinions and judge—something we are certainly adept at doing.

The sages teach us that if a thought excludes others, it does not represent the truth. Why? Because it excludes totality. Truth is the sum of all parts that comprise a topic, a thought, or a situation. The Hebrew word for truth is *Emet (אמת)* composed of three letters: *Alef (א), Mem* (מ), and *Tav* (ת). They correspond to the first, middle, and last letters of the Hebrew Alphabet, indicating that truth contains everything: the beginning, middle, and end. For something to be true, it must encompass everything it entails. Rejecting what does not fit into your mind keeps you in a limited perspective, distancing you away from truth.

We live according to a thought system that is becoming obsolete and that most of us do not know how to escape. However, by becoming aware of this, we can begin to change it.

In the last hundred years, we have advanced technologically more than in the previous two thousand years of civilization. My wife's grandmother, for example, didn't have a refrigerator in her childhood; she kept food cold in an underground cellar dug outside her house and traveled by horse-drawn cart. During her lifetime, she witnessed humanity's arrival on the moon and now uses an iPad and ChatGPT. Technological advancement goes hand in hand with the development of consciousness; as consciousness evolves, so does science. They are components of a whole, moving forward in parallel.

In recent times, consciousness has experienced a great awakening, as has science. Both are moving at unimaginable speeds, forcing us to adapt to a new rhythm. For years, the teachings of Kabbalah remained hidden from the public, taught selectively from master to student. Today, these teachings have become public, coinciding with the greatest scientific advancements in history.

Although the wisdom of Kabbalah emerged with creation itself and will accompany us until the end of time, I recognize that the forms and explanations in this book are valid for this moment and may become obsolete over time. Just because an idea is true does not mean it is THE TRUTH.

FLAT LIKE A SOCCER FIELD - SPHERICAL LIKE A BALL

The *Zohar*, the central book of Kabbalah, written over two thousand years ago, addressed revolutionary concepts for its time in its particular language. Therefore, it is crucial to break free from the limitations of our minds to comprehend this wisdom. What do I mean by this? Let's look at these verses from the *Zohar*:

Vayikra: Verse 141 "Rav Hamnuna Saba (the elder) explains further in his book that the entire inhabited land rolls around like a ball, so that some are up, and some are down. NAMELY, THE CREATURES AROUND THE GLOBE ARE OPPOSITE TO EACH OTHER AND THE SEVEN SECTIONS OF THE GLOBE ARE SEVEN LANDS. All the creatures OF SIX OF THE LANDS are different in their appearance according to the difference in the atmosphere in each place, and they live like any other man."

Vayikra: Verse 142 "There is an inhabited place, so that when there is light on some—ON THAT SIDE OF THE GLOBE—it is dark for others ON THE OTHER SIDE OF THE WORLD. THUS, when it is day for one group, it is night for the others. There is an inhabited place where there is day only and no night, save for a little while."

In these verses, the *Zohar,* well ahead of its time, proclaimed that the Earth is spherical, rotates like a ball, and comprises seven continents. It also mentions time zones, indicating that while it is day in some places, it is night in others. Furthermore, the *Zohar* knows that in Antarctica, during one season of the year, it is all day, and during another all night—something that was only confirmed much later through modern exploration.

About five hundred and fifty years ago, outside of the elite and educated population, many people still firmly believed that the Earth was flat, like a soccer field. Today, approximately 1% of the world's population still holds this belief. However, the vast majority accept that the Earth is round, similar to a soccer ball.

If you are thinking, "Of course, the Earth isn't flat—those people were wrong, and I am right because it is round," you have just played into the game I have been explaining. Remember that Galileo Galilei, for instance, was condemned for asserting that the Earth orbits around the sun. People were so convinced they possessed the truth that any other possibility had to be eliminated. Today, we experience the Earth as flat to the naked eye, but we understand it as spherical based on the scientific evidence we have. However, what is truly important here is not the shape of the Earth but how we perceive and accept ideas.

Conflict arises when we believe our perception is the only truth, leaving no space for other possibilities. How often do we act toward others with a narrow mindset, like flat-earthers, voicing opinions without evidence and making assumptions suited to our convenience?

Recently, while watching my son's soccer game, the parent sitting next to me said, "I'm going to move into the shade; the sun has shifted and it's burning me." I pointed out that it is the Earth that is moving, not the sun. He hesitated for a moment, smiled, and moved to the shade anyway. From his perspective, the sun was moving, even though he knew it was the opposite.

Recognizing life's paradoxes and embracing multiple perspectives brings us closer to reality than holding on to a narrow viewpoint. Each person sees and experiences a different reality that does not include that of others. That is how we humans are—at least until now.

What do you see here? We are only capable of perceiving one number at a time. We cannot see both sides of a coin simultaneously, so we become convinced that what we see is the whole truth. Instead of truly thinking, what we tend to do is simply express our thoughts. We love to share opinions and pass judgment because thinking involves a complex cognitive process that allows us to integrate and accept new ideas. In contrast, sharing opinions and judging keep us clinging to what is familiar and rejecting anything that threatens us or challenges what we refuse to accept.

One of the greatest demonstrations of wisdom is humility regarding what we believe to be true, knowing that we will never see with absolute clarity. Question everything, even your thoughts. This does not mean that your perspective or the truths you hold are weak, but keep in mind that you can only see the part you are conscious of, shaped by your own biases. Challenge the things you are certain about and test if they still hold up.

WHAT'S THE POINT?

Our senses are the tools we use to interact with the world around us. However, the *Zohar* tells us that the perception we gain from our five senses is, in reality, an illusion.

Illusionists are true masters of the art of manipulation. During their performances, you witness how they skillfully manage to alter your perception of reality. A good magician constantly plays with the limitations of your five senses, leading you to doubt what is happening. They understand that your mind desperately seeks explanations—not because it needs the truth, but because it needs things to make sense.

In everyday life, the same thing happens, with the difference that we go through the world believing we are in the presence of reality. What we perceive through our senses is not the totality of what truly is, but only a limited fraction. Actual reality lies beyond what our senses perceive.

Let us look at some examples.

You might perceive your favorite soccer team's jersey as blue. However, science explains that what's really happening is that light absorbs all colors and reflects only blue when it hits the fabric. That's why you see it that way—it is precisely the color the fabric 'rejected.' In fact, you could say the uniform is every color except blue, even though that's exactly what your eyes perceive.

One of my favorite examples is video, where the perception of movement is an illusion. In one second of film footage, twenty-four frames are projected (currently, in digital video, this number is much higher). These images pass one by one so quickly that they create the illusion of movement. What we are seeing, in reality, are individual images that follow one after another, and our eyes and brains, limited in their processing capacity, interpret this rapid flow as continuous movement.

Similarly, our hearing is not capable of perceiving the full spectrum of sound waves that we know exist. For instance, dogs hear sounds that we do not perceive. We also know that, at this very moment, there are radio waves present in the room with you that you cannot hear—at least not without a device that can capture them and reproduce them at a frequency compatible with your auditory system. Not being able to hear them does not mean they are not in your room in this instant or that they do not exist.

Imagine you are playing a soccer match, standing before the opponent's goal, ready to shoot. Your leg does not move on its own to kick the ball; in reality, it is the result of internal factors influencing that action. First, the desire to score a goal is driven by your motivation to win the game. This desire is accompanied by thoughts that arise in your mind to help you achieve that objective. You visualize the movement you need to make, calculate the force and direction of the shot, take a breath, and finally decide to kick the ball. Behind that movement, which seems simple and spontaneous, a complex process operates without our full awareness. Every movement we make in the physical world is preceded by an internal cause that initiates it.

Physical manifestation, that is, everything we perceive in the material world—results from prior causes operating on a deeper, more subtle level.

Our senses perceive only the effects, not the causes.

Kabbalists teach that the universe operates under the law of cause and effect: every action generates a corresponding reaction in our lives. Time, however, introduces a space that gives us the opportunity to correct and complete our actions.

Imagine a soccer match where two players are expelled from the field at the slightest contact. Or if the coach removed a player every time they lost the ball on their first play. It would be chaos. Similarly, think about training at the gym: during the first week of weightlifting, you are unlikely to notice significant changes. The second week, neither. In the third week, you might still not see much progress, which could make you doubt the results and demotivate you from continuing.

A period is necessary for causes to manifest in this world. Just as a game requires time and space for players to develop on the field, this phase allows us to make mistakes, learn, and accumulate experiences. It is in that intermediate space where the true process of growth and learning unfolds, allowing our experiences to integrate and transform into wisdom.

This separation between cause and effect, along with our inability to see their connection, makes us forget that the actions we perceive with our senses did not arise on their own, nor are they the product of chance. There is a hidden cause behind them.

Let's consider another example: if you hold a soccer ball in your hands, you cannot perceive the entire process behind its creation. You only see the final product. In fact,

I bet you are thinking right now that you have no idea how a ball is made. Behind a soccer ball, there is a complex process of design, material selection, stitching, valve insertion, painting, inflation, quality testing, and distribution. With our senses, we simply connect with the result: a ball.

We have simply mentioned a few examples where our five senses fall short of providing us with complete information about reality, as we understand it to exist. Our senses, being limited tools that show us only a manifested state of things, do not offer us clarity to determine what is true and beneficial for us and what might not be. However, that is not where it ends; this situation becomes even more complicated.

Not only do our senses deceive us, but so does our perception. How often have you looked for your glasses only to realize you were wearing them? Or searched for a cap in a drawer ten times until you finally found it in that same place, not understanding why you did not see it the previous nine times? Have you ever placed your phone in the refrigerator and walked out with yogurt in your hand?

Our perception of the world is shaped by numerous factors—not only by our limited senses but also by our environment: who our family is, where we grew up, which school we attended, and who our friends are, among many other factors.

As if that weren't enough, and to make the game even more interesting, we have emotions that play a significant role on the field. You might feel fear, anxiety, frustration, enthusiasm, excitement, etc., depending on the state of the game and your personal expectations. These emotions influence how you act and perform on the field. How you manage your feelings determines how you resolve most conflicts.

When a referee awards a penalty, various interpretations of their decision arise. Everyone defends their perspective, sometimes even to the point of violence. Our thoughts lead us to believe that the world is precisely as we see and think it is. If we believe our thoughts show us reality and accept it as such, then so it will be for you.

If your life experience were complete, without setbacks, and you made the best decisions at every moment, this world of illusion would not present a challenge. What does it matter if you do not see reality if you are happy, fulfilled, and at peace? However, the reality of our daily lives is usually not like this. That is why the following question arises: How can we transcend our limitations and connect with the causes of existence? This way, we will be able to see beyond the constraints of our senses and reconcile the paradoxes inherent in our limited physical perception.

THE SENTENCE BELOW IS TRUE.

THE SENTENCE ABOVE IS FALSE.

LET'S BUILD A STADIUM

The *Torah* (the five books of the Hebrew Bible) begins by recounting the creation of the world: *"In the **beginning,** God created the **Heavens** and the **Earth**."*

- **The Beginning** refers to the **creation** of **time**
- **The Heavens** refers to the **creation of space**
- **The Earth** refers to the **creation** of **matter**

The physical world we inhabit is defined by the dimensions of time, space, and matter. The Torah, with just seven words in Hebrew and ten in the English translation, explains the act of creation in a way that is accessible to all while simultaneously offering multiple layers of depth for those who wish to explore further.

The Torah begins with the word *Bereshit* (בְּרֵאשִׁית), translated into English as "In the beginning." The *Zohar* offers seventy explanations for this word, but let us focus on one. The word *Bereshit* can be divided into two parts: *Bet* and *Reshit*. *Bet* represents the number two in the Hebrew alphabet, and *Reshit* means "beginning." The Torah teaches us that there are two creations: a first beginning that corresponds to the spiritual world, or the world of causes, and a second beginning corresponding to the physical world, or the world of consequences.

In the story of creation, all elements are mentioned twice. For example, on the first day, The Light appears, and on the fourth day, the creation of the sun is mentioned. Since the only light we know is sunlight, and without the sun, there would be no concept of days and nights, how then could the Torah speak of days when the sun had not been created until the fourth day? Because as mentioned earlier, there are two creations—one spiritual and one physical. In Kabbalah, it is taught that Light was not created; it has always existed, as it is infinite. It is the source of all existence and the origin of everything we know. At the beginning of creation, Light did not appear from nothing—it just revealed itself.

There exists the world of causes and the world of consequences. Creation introduced the illusion of space to separate these two realms, allowing the existence of a physical world where creation can unfold. This division enables us to recognize ourselves through our separation from one another. In this way, I can perceive "myself here" and "you there," creating a space between us that makes connection and interaction possible.

Imagine an imposing mountain; using a shovel, you separate a piece from it. Now, that piece is recognized as a stone. What is the difference between the stone and the mountain? Is there truly a distinction between them? They are composed of the same material and part of the same whole; only now is there a space between them. If we remove that space, the stone will be reunited with the mountain, and there will no longer be any difference between them. Similarly, the creation of the world gave rise to space so that we can recognize each other.

We can't give if there is no one to receive, nor can we play soccer without an opposing team. The Creation is an illusion that distorts oneness, creating an apparent separation that gives rise to human experience as we perceive it.

A professional soccer field is approximately 100 meters long and 50 meters wide, yet only twenty-two players are on the field. If the players were placed side by side, they would cover approximately 1% of the total field area. This vast empty space allows them to move and develop their game. It is what allows free will so you can decide where to go.

Let's consider another example where space is crucial. If we removed the space between words in this book, we would optimize the number of pages and save paper in its printed version, but it would likely be difficult to read. The same would happen if we did not pause when speaking. You would save time on what you say, but communication would not be clear.

The illusion of space and time in our physical world allows us to advance, overcome challenges, learn, experience, and achieve goals.

The ease with which someone can play a soccer video game says more about the skill of the game's creator than about the player's intelligence.

TIKKUN OR CORRECTION

*Tikkun**, which in Hebrew means "correction," refers to the process of spiritual refinement that we are all destined to undergo in this world. It is a central concept in Kabbalah, as it is the way the Creator designed for His players to achieve worthiness and ultimately win this game of life.

Our *Tikkun* refers to all the personal aspects we are destined to correct. How can we identify our *Tikkun*? Take a moment to reflect on what makes you feel uncomfortable or frustrated. Observe the patterns that repeat in your life and the actions of others that cause you pain or discomfort. It is through these experiences that you can find clues about what you need to correct.

Every situation is a life lesson, and each moment is a precious opportunity to fulfill a part of our *Tikkun*. Being ready to recognize life's challenges is crucial for fully seizing these opportunities. Even if we choose not to face these challenges and instead flee from our *Tikkun*, it is essential to understand that every action—whether aimed at fulfilling or avoiding our correction—has been considered since the beginning of creation. Life operates according to the divine laws of cause and effect, and in the end, only we are responsible for our actions and their consequences.

The *Tikkun* is the reason the stadium was created, soccer was invented, all its rules were established, and why hundreds of teams and millions of players exist. This is why we are all playing, striving, and sweating on the field.

Think about your most significant achievements. Have you noticed how they are always accompanied by challenges that you have had to overcome? Life's obstacles are, in truth, disguised opportunities that help you complete your *Tikkun*. Every challenge you overcome allows you to correct some aspect of your *Tikkun*, bringing you closer to your goal.

When we refine ourselves by overcoming obstacles, we complete an aspect of our *Tikkun*, which is the key to moving forward in life. Often, we fail to recognize difficulties as opportunities and instead label them as adverse events that we fall victim to. We avoid facing uncomfortable situations, and as a result, we are unable to learn what they are meant to teach us. Life's challenges 'pinch' our *Tikkun*, keeping us alert and showing where our work lies. Numerous situations that come into our lives are beyond our control; they are external to us. However, what does belong to us and what we are responsible for is how we react to these situations, how we interpret them, and what we learn from them.

Rejecting the adversity you're facing is like assuming the universe made a mistake with you in that moment, failing to realize that this situation didn't happen to you, but happened FOR YOU. This is why we often perceive difficulties as "bad." If we stopped rejecting them and instead allowed ourselves to live through them—since they're happening anyway—maybe we could make the most of what they've come to teach us.

The true victory in the game of life is not measured by external achievements, but by the depth of our inner transformation and the love we are capable of giving and receiving. By accepting this challenge and choosing to step onto the field to play, we discover the true meaning of our existence and align ourselves with the divine purpose that guides us all.

Life indeed confronts us with intense and unpleasant moments. When these moments occur, resisting, denying, and wishing they would not happen puts us at odds with what we are meant to experience. It resembles a situation in soccer when a defender approaches, and instead of attempting a move or dribbling the ball, you choose not to kick and disengage from the game, ending up frustrated for not even trying. Or it is like saying, "Let's play, but only if you pass me the ball the way I want," then asking the defender to take three steps back because you don't want him so close, while also reminding him of the push from last time and emphasizing that such behavior is not how the game should be played.

Instead of experiencing the life you have, you desire life to be as you believe it should be, attempting to control the uncontrollable. This leads to frustration, as life is as it is, not as our limited mind wishes it to be. Resisting these experiences means losing the opportunity to learn and elevate ourselves.

Accepting each moment as it is allows us to transform even the most challenging situations into opportunities for growth and to reveal the Divine Light in our lives.

“I am as successful

as the level of risk

I am willing to take”.

David Copperfield

GOD, LIGHT, AND THE INFINITE

In the current era, advances in science and technology have enabled us to explore and understand previously unimaginable phenomena. We have reached surprising levels of understanding in different areas of existence due to quantum physics, satellites, and artificial intelligence. Today, we can explain the subatomic world, have mobile devices with unlimited data access, and employ artificial intelligence capable of understanding complex instructions, generating images, writing texts, and engaging in real-time conversations almost indistinguishable from those of humans.

Despite these advances, we continue to perceive the world as solid and compact. However, the reality is quite different. Atoms, the fundamental building blocks of all matter, reveal that what we consider solid is, in fact, an illusion.

If we imagine the atoms as the building blocks that make up everything around us, and if this brick were the size of a soccer stadium, its nucleus would be like a whistle placed at the center of the field. Meanwhile, the electrons would be tiny particles moving around the perimeter of the stadium. In fact, atoms are made up of particles that occupy very little space, which we understand as essentially energy moving at incredibly high speeds. At the subatomic level, we can say that our world is composed of 1% energy in motion and 99% empty space.

In Kabbalistic terms, it is explained that the physical world represents only 1% of the reality we perceive, while the world of causes, beyond what we can perceive with our senses, represents the remaining 99%.

Both science and Kabbalah agree that we can only experience 1% of reality. The sages had this knowledge centuries ago, but the world was not ready to assimilate it until science could demonstrate it.

Although this space appears empty to the naked eye, Kabbalah suggests that this 99% is filled with consciousness, which accompanies creation and makes possible the complex game in which we live. This consciousness is the force that sustains and gives meaning to everything that exists in our physical world.

According to the wisdom of Kabbalah, what we perceive through our five senses—what we see, touch, hear, taste, and smell—makes up only a small part of reality. This limited level of perception is referred to as the "Tree of Knowledge" and represents just 1% of what truly exists.

The remaining 99% belongs to the non-physical world, a deeper, invisible dimension that Kabbalah calls the "Tree of Life," made up of ten levels of spiritual energy known as the Sefirot.

Just as we cannot directly connect to a power plant or approach the sun, we cannot receive the Creator's Light directly. It is like trying to play in the World Cup when we barely know how to kick a ball and have not gone through the necessary process to compete at a professional level. In this world, we have a system that helps us access Infinite Light without being burned by its intensity: the Sefirot.

The ten Sefirot are luminous emanations that connect us with the 99%—the unseen world we want to consciously engage with to access and influence our lives at the level of causes. The Infinite Light that emanates through the Sefirot is the source of fulfillment within reach of all who connect with it.

Similarly, electricity—an invisible form of energy to the human eye without a defined course—responds to specific laws and can be used in various ways. Both the Sefirot and electricity must be channeled from their source, where they originate and exist in a potential state, and undergo a process to manifest on a physical level allowing us to benefit from them. Thus, it is the same electricity used to illuminate a soccer stadium, power a lawn mower, or drive speakers. The primary source of electricity is always the same. However, we must transform this energy into an appropriate voltage and use equipment designed for that purpose, depending on how we intend to use it.

Kabbalists describe the Divine Light as the infinite consciousness that manifests and gives rise to the existence of our world. This process resembles the phenomenon of a crystal prism that receives light at one end and refracts it into seven distinct colors at the other. Similarly, The Light of creation is channeled toward our physical plane through the Sefirot.

In Kabbalah, "The Light" refers to the divine emanation of the Infinite within our reality. Our five senses allow us to perceive aspects of life where God's creation manifests, but not its essence. We can appreciate the created world but not fully comprehend the intelligence behind its creation. Attempting to define God leads us to lose ourselves in his infinitude, while aspiring to reach Him reflects His greatness. If you believe you have understood Him, you are deceiving yourself. God is the ultimate paradox of existence, a reality that transcends all human comprehension and definition. God surpasses existence itself, which can cause cognitive dissonance—as accepting that any understanding we have of God is inherently limited and, therefore, false presents a profound challenge for the human mind.

There is the perception that each religion, and even each individual, believes in a different God, with some going so far as to claim that theirs is the only true one. Others think they believe in God but only in the one they conceive, rejecting the existence of all others who, according to them, do not exist. They fail to understand that diversity in interpretations reflects the grandeur of the whole, which manifests in the physical world through various expressions. This diversity does not divide; what divides is our limited perception.

Instead, it is essential to open ourselves to an infinite number of perspectives on divinity and understand that everything we see, think, and imagine—across the billions of people who exist now, who have existed, and who will exist—is only a part of God's expression. This understanding invites us to expand our consciousness and embrace the diversity of experiences and beliefs as facets of a much greater truth, which, although we aspire to achieve, is essentially unattainable.

Kabbalah is more concerned in how we relate to and approach God than in speculating about His nature. Thus, your conception of God, or the absence of one, reveals more about you than divinity itself. In fact, we do not find systematic "proofs" of God's existence in the Zohar or in other Kabbalistic texts. We find teachings and practices that enable profound changes in consciousness, bringing us closer to the Divine. The true wisdom of Kabbalah lies in internal transformation and openness to the divine experience beyond the limitations of our intellectual understanding. Instead of seeking external proof, Kabbalah guides us toward an inner search, where what we discover within determines what we can experience outside. The ultimate purpose of Kabbalah is not to solve the mysteries of the universe intellectually or philosophically, but to transform our consciousness and our being.

The *Ein Sof** (in Hebrew, "without end") is a term used in Kabbalistic language to refer to the boundless infinite—the all-encompassing that transcends any limit or definition. Kabbalists also mention different types of luminous emanations within our reach, which serve as pathways to connect with The Light that emanates from the infinite. The existence of various types of lights, emanations, and even different names assigned to God does not imply any separation in divine reality and unity. Rather, this reflects the limits of human perception in fully connecting with the Creator of the infinite.

It is important to note that Kabbalists do not usually use the word *God* in their writings for all the reasons mentioned above. Therefore, I will choose to use it sparingly. Instead, I will refer to terms that evoke the infinite and luminous nature of the Creator to better guide our spiritual exploration.

Achieving closeness and connection with the Creator's Infinite Light requires effort. It is not enough to be a spectator, even an active one full of opinions. As in soccer, you do not learn to play simply by watching from the sidelines. We must step onto the field and commit to a series of daily exercises that allow us, over time, to advance in our spiritual growth and our connection with this Infinite Light. That is why, according to Kabbalah, there is a form of training consisting of 613 exercises called the 613 *Mitzvot**.

The 613 *Mitzvot* are connections or precepts that derive from the Torah. The *Mitzvot* encompass aspects of life such as the relationship with God, ritual practices, personal and social ethics, and civil laws. If you add the digits that make up 613 (6 + 1 + 3), you get 10, which confirms that the path of the Torah serves as a bridge of connection to the ten Sefirot.

According to Talmud Tractate Makkot 23b–24a, there is a profound relationship that reveals itself when we look at the division of the 613 precepts of the Torah. These are split into 365 negative precepts (actions to avoid) and 248 positive precepts (actions to perform). This division is not coincidental. The 365 negative precepts correspond to the **365 days** of the year, while the 248 positive precepts correspond to the **248 limbs** of the human body. This connection highlights the alignment between spiritual and physical existence.

Furthermore, we can observe a parallel in the cosmos: 365 is the number of days it takes the Earth (Malchut*) to complete its orbit, while 248 is the number of years it takes Pluto (Keter*) to complete its orbit. This cosmic connection further emphasizes the harmony between the divine design of the universe and the teachings of the Torah.

Keter and Malchut, the first and last of the Sefirot, respectively, show us that everything is part of a united whole: the planets above and the grass of the soccer field down here on Earth. All creation contains the ten Sefirot. How is this possible? Because the Sefirot are the DNA that harbors the spiritual essence—the consciousness behind all creation.

“There is no commandment that does not include within it the Ten Sefirot”.

Zohar Ki Tetze, chapter 57.

ICONIC PLAYERS

Kabbalah is a mystical wisdom that originated within Judaism, seeking to understand and experience the nature of the Creator as it manifests in this world, as well as the laws of the universe and the human soul. Through its teachings and practices along with the study of various writings—its central text, the *Zohar*—Kabbalah, offers a spiritual perspective of the world. It invites us to transform our lives through the knowledge and application of its teachings. It is a guide for those who seek not only to comprehend the mystery of existence and know the soul of the *Torah* but also for those who yearn to achieve a state of harmony and personal fulfillment.

The word *Kabbalah* (קַבָּלָה) means "to receive" (from the Hebrew *lekabel*). This translation reveals a profound teaching: on one level, Kabbalah instructs us on how to receive The Light in every situation so that it can manifest in our lives. However, Kabbalah also implies learning to receive and accept life's circumstances as they unfold. This understanding allows us to cultivate an attitude of receptivity and openness that enables the Divine Light to manifest through us.

The information in this book derives from the study of the *Zohar*, whose name is translated as "Splendor." This text is a compilation of mystical teachings, commentaries, and allegorical stories about the *Torah*, originally written in Aramaic. The authorship of the *Zohar* is primarily attributed to the 2nd-century mystical sage Rabbi Shimon Bar Yochai*. However, the final composition of the text is credited to the 13th-century Spanish rabbi Moses de León*.

The *Zohar* is presented in dialogues and narratives between characters who discuss spiritual, cosmological, and ethical topics from a mystical perspective, offering profound insights. It explores concepts such as the *Sefirot*, creation, the nature of the soul, and the relationship between the Creator and His universe.

Subsequently, this wisdom remained hidden and was taught only directly from master to student. About five hundred years ago, one of the most renowned Kabbalists to date, Rabbi Isaac Luria* (known as "the *Arizal*"), created a methodology for the study and understanding of the *Zohar* and Kabbalah, which he captured in his work, *The Writings of the Arizal.*

Less than a hundred years ago, Rav Yehuda Ashlag* (1885–1954), known as Baal HaSulam*, explained the *Zohar* and translated it from Aramaic to Hebrew. In his work *HaSulam* ("The Ladder"), he added detailed explanations that make these texts more accessible and comprehensible. Additionally, he wrote the *Talmud Eser Sefirot** ("The Study of the Ten Sefirot"), a fundamental work in teaching modern Kabbalah.

Today, Kabbalah has become a spiritual teaching accessible to the public, transcending its mystical Jewish origin to attract a diverse audience. Several modern Kabbalists agree that there is an urgent need to spread this knowledge to prepare humanity for the times we live in.

There are various methods of studying the *Sefirot*, such as the approach of the Kabbalist Moses Cordovero* However, the Arizal's methodology is the most recognized and studied today.

THE SEFIROT

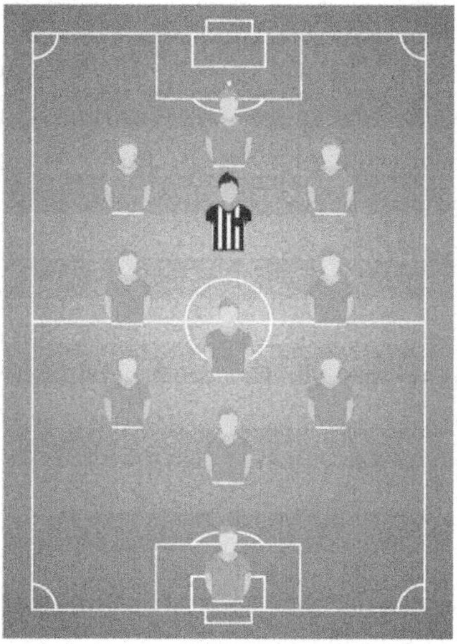

ALIGNMENT OF THE SEFIROT
IN THE TREE OF LIFE

ALIGNMENT OF PLAYERS
ON THE SOCCER FIELD

Is it just me, or is there a certain resemblance between these two images?

The "Tree of Life" is a central framework to Kabbalah teachings. It is more than just a simple graphic representation of the Sefirot; these are divine emanations whereby the world was created, and through which Infinite Light flows into this physical plane. The Tree of Life represents the world of causes and provides a structure to connect the divine with the earthly, thus allowing us to attain fulfillment in our lives. The Sefirot serve to elevate and connect this physical reality with the spiritual dimension.

Each Sefirah* (singular of Sefirot) represents a divine aspect or attribute, each with its own meaning and function within the Tree of Life. These dimensions not only channel The Light but also influence our life experience as we receive their energy. The Tree of Life structure also includes a series of paths that connect the Sefirot, representing the relationships and flows of divine energy between them.

The Sefirot act as veils that gradually attenuate the intensity of The Light emanating from the *Ein Sof* (infinite world) as it descends into the physical plane. This process of Light gradation allows us to receive it in a way we can handle.

When The Light descends to our physical world (*Malchut*), its radiance is concealed to such an extent that we are unable to perceive it. This process of attenuation and concealment of The Light is fundamental to our spiritual growth. It offers us the opportunity to work through challenges and overcome them, enabling us to deserve and truly earn the Infinite Light in our lives and ultimately lead a state of fulfillment and spiritual perfection. Only through the effort required in the revelation of The Light and by facing challenging situations can we truly appreciate and savor the wholeness that comes with having earned it.

The Sefirot are divine manifestations that reflect the inner qualities we must correct. However, we cannot correct something that is not intrinsically ours. Therefore, in life, we do not aspire to change who we are but to refine, cleanse, and reactivate qualities that belong to us and yet remain dormant or trapped in darkness. By perfecting ourselves, we return to being the complete and luminous beings we have always been. Attempting to change suggests abandoning oneself to become someone else, which is impossible, as our essence is something we cannot detach from.

Take, for instance, a player who stands out as one of soccer's brightest stars. When he was a child and decided to learn soccer, he was not acquiring an entirely new skill but connecting with an innate talent, a dormant potential he chose to manifest and perfect. If this soccer star had tried to practice another sport that didn't align with his natural abilities, such as padel or javelin throw, he would never have achieved the same level of success because it was not an innate quality he possessed. In the game of life, we seek to reconnect with our essence, awakening The Light that already resides within us, which is waiting to be discovered so it can shine in all its splendor.

The *Zohar* explains: "As above, so below," indicating that "above" is where the cause of the physical world originates—the 99% where the celestial worlds exist, beyond the reach of the five senses. "Below" refers to the physical world of the 1%, which is nothing more than a reflection, a manifestation of the world above.

Just as Kabbalah reveals to us the structure of the Tree of Life through the ten Sefirot to help us understand how existence manifests in the world, modern science explains it through its theories and discoveries. The resemblance between the two remains astonishing.

Today, string theory[1] is one of the leading scientific proposals about a "theory of everything" that seeks to unify all the forces and particles in the universe.

[1] String theory is a theoretical physics framework that suggests fundamental particles are one-dimensional strings. The different vibrations of these strings correspond to different particles. The theory attempts to unify gravity with quantum mechanics. It is considered a "theory of everything" that describes all fundamental forces and particles in the universe within a single and coherent framework. String theory requires a universe of ten dimensions to be consistent with nature.

Although it remains a developing theory and faces many challenges, it offers an exciting and profound perspective on the fundamental nature of reality. This perspective resonates astonishingly with the teachings explained in Kabbalah over two thousand years ago. Here, I very briefly outline the basic postulates of string theory and, in parentheses, highlight the connections I draw with the explanations presented in Kabbalah.

This theory proposes that the universe is composed of vibrating strings and that these strings function only within a ten-dimensional system. Of these, there are three spatial dimensions (Keter, Chochmah*, and Binah*) and one temporal (Malchut). While the remaining six dimensions (*Zeir Anpin**) are hidden—compacted within a complex manner and not directly perceptible

The similarity and precision between both explanations are truly impressive. These comparisons illustrate how two fields of knowledge separated by thousands of years are increasingly converging in their approaches and discoveries.

Although the Sefirot are, in fact, a single indivisible unit, we will group them into three categories to better understand them according to their qualities and influences:

Arich Anpin* (Intellectual Sefirot): *Keter, Chochmah, and Binah.*
Zeir Anpin (Emotional Sefirot): Chesed*, Gevurah*, Tiferet*, Netzach*, Hod*, Yesod*.
Malchut: Represents the physical world as we know it.

Arich Anpin: The first set of three Sefirot represents the highest divine consciousness that emanates from the Creator's Light. Composed of Keter, Chochmah, and Binah, *Arich Anpin* translates as "Long Face." These Sefirot are closest to the Source of Creation and have no direct reference to anything physical. They exist outside the playing field and intervene from beyond the framework of what we perceive with our senses on the physical plane, guiding the divine will in this world.

Zeir Anpin: Comprises six Sefirot: Chesed, Gevurah, Tiferet, Netzach, Hod, and Yesod. *Zeir Anpin* represents the "Small Face," or the emotional and spiritual dimensions that mediate between the higher emanations and the physical world. It serves as a channel through which the divine influences of the higher Sefirot are filtered and prepared to manifest on the physical plane.

Malchut: This is the tenth and final Sefirah, representing the physical world as we know it. It is the manifestation of all the influences and energies that descend through the other Sefirot, ultimately materializing in our tangible reality.

The general rules for understanding soccer are well known, just like the physical laws explained by science. Now, we will explore some of the fundamental principles governing this invisible world, as explained through Kabbalah, and examine their practical applications in our lives.

Let us begin by exploring each Sefirah one by one, starting with Keter.

KETER

Keter means "crown" in Hebrew and is the first Sefirah in the Tree of Life. It represents pure potential, the original source that encompasses everything. At the level of Keter, there is no manifestation whatsoever, as it represents maximum potential.

In the world, nothing happens without the vital energy of Keter that sustains it. Keter is compared to the primary essential consciousness behind the idea that gave rise to soccer and includes all the elements derived from it, such as rules, plays, teams, championships, and more.

Keter resembles a seed that encloses all the potential information of a tree, from the number of roots to the fruits, branches, and leaves it will develop throughout its life. No manifestation of a tree can differ from the seed that gave it life. An apple tree will never produce mangoes, as its essence and DNA are that of an apple tree.

Just as we cannot benefit from a seed until it develops and bears fruit, we need Keter to manifest to receive its benefits in the physical world. The seed must remain hidden underground for the transformation that will lead it to become a tree. Similarly, Keter remains concealed until its process of manifestation begins. As the seed grows and transforms into a tree, our ability to influence the result diminishes. The purity of our desires and thoughts represents Keter in any activity we engage in, determining the outcome of our actions.

Keter is the thought behind the thought, encompassing everything in a state of pure potential. Once Keter gives life to a creation, it merges into it and disappears, which is why it is sometimes not mentioned among the Sefirot.

Keter teaches us that even when you feel like a king by scoring the winning goal in a final, you must remember that every king wears a crown on his head. Without a crown, there is no king. Though the euphoria of the moment may make you believe that you alone scored the winning goal, remember that something above you allowed that experience and orchestrated everything without being seen. Keter is always active, giving life at every moment and every second of existence.

Another helpful analogy to understand the first Sefirah, Keter, is that of a video game you download onto your console. The compressed file—before it's even installed—already contains all possible plays, teams, and movements. There is no action you can take that is not already programmed into that original file. Yet until it is installed, all that potential remains in a latent state—one you cannot interact with yet.

If a video game were to stop working for just a few seconds on the console, it would instantly disappear from your screen because the source that gives it life would stop feeding it. Similarly, the energy of Keter is constantly giving life to existence, merging into it to ensure its continuity. Life would cease to exist if, even for a single second, the energy of Keter stopped emanating. Life is being created in every instant—it is an eternal present moment.

CHOCHMAH

Chochmah, translated as "wisdom," comes from the Hebrew words *koach* ("strength") and *mah* ("what?"), symbolizing the power of the question—the foundation of all wisdom.

Imagine you are the creator of soccer, having just conceived the brilliant idea of this amazing game. What would be the next step after conceiving the idea? You would need to shape it, define the game's objective and establish all its rules.

Chochmah could be considered the complete conception of the game, including its rules. These rules are intangible yet enable the creation of the game and help us begin to understand it. Nothing can exist outside of Chochmah, for without it, it would no longer be soccer. A player cannot ignore a rule simply because they cannot see, touch, feel, smell, or taste it. That would be absurd, as this structure gives soccer its meaning, organizes the ideas, and guides the players.

The Light of Chochmah is associated with the beginning of thought, with the desire to offer everything you have without expecting anything in return—simply for the sake of sharing. This concept of giving for the sake of giving represents a profound level of consciousness, an affinity with the Infinite Light that simply IS and simply GIVES without diminishing itself in the act. Therefore, it lacks nothing.

The consciousness level of giving solely for the sake of giving is foreign to human nature, which tends to want to receive without necessarily deserving. The experience of parenthood brings us closer to the Chochmah level of consciousness, as it allows us to love someone more than ourselves and experience this level of giving unconditionally.

Chochmah is associated with paternal and masculine energy that gives life, creates, protects, and establishes norms. This energy provides structure and support, while exercising authority.

We speak of Chochmah as an energy with positive polarity and masculine characteristics. While this energy is associated with masculinity on the physical plane, it does not necessarily refer to human beings. We should not confuse the association of energy and polarity with what we know in the physical world, assuming that only a man can establish rules, protect, or manifest masculine energy.

When we reach the level of Chochmah, all our desires are completely fulfilled. This is because Chochmah is so close to the light emanating from the source that it lacks nothing.

Let's do the following exercise. Do you feel a cramp in your leg right now? I hope not. Do you wish not to have a cramp in your leg? Of course. However, were you aware throughout the day that you didn't want to feel that pain? Probably not. The desire to be free of pain was completely fulfilled. When a desire is fully satisfied, it does not manifest in our consciousness.

Rav Ashlag teaches that light is the only thing that truly exists and, therefore, is the only source capable of fully satisfying our desires. Moreover, a desire can awaken in us if only we have previously experienced its fulfillment. Therefore, it is not our desire that allows The Light to enter our lives; instead, it is The Light itself that, having filled us before, awakens in us the yearning to experience it again.

The fulfillment we seek is something we have already known before. Our desires are not random; they are linked to past experiences in which we have connected with the Divine Light. The desires we feel reflect the skills and areas we have developed or aspire to perfect in this life.

To understand this better, imagine you are at halftime during a soccer match, entering the locker room feeling thirsty. You might think that thirst is the reason you desire water, and that drinking is the way to quench that desire. However, you would not be able to desire water if you had never tasted it first. The desire arises because we have already experienced the satisfaction of drinking water in the past. This same principle applies to all our desires; they are activated due to previous experiences of satisfaction and connection with The Light.

Our desires guide us toward our goals and connect us with our latent potential, waiting to be manifested and perfected. By recognizing and refining these desires, we set ourselves on the path to revealing our true essence and achieving spiritual fulfillment.

Thus, from Chochmah unfolds a force of feminine polarity, whose role is to receive and develop the divine fullness that flows from the endless desire to give. This stage is known as Binah, and it represents the next step in the spiritual process.

BINAH

Binah, the third Sefirah, along with Keter and Chochmah, constitutes what is known in Kabbalah as *Arich Anpin* ("Long Face"). Binah, defined as 'understanding,' represents the active process of learning and comprehension. It is an energy of feminine polarity, and its name includes the Hebrew word *Ben*, which means 'son.' As a feminine energy, Binah has the capacity to give birth and nurture with the passion that characterizes a mother. For a mother to conceive, she needs a seed (Keter) and a masculine figure, a giver (Chochmah). From this union, Binah can conceive, develop, and bring forth creation.

After the great idea of soccer (Keter), where we already have all the rules (Chochmah), the next step is to internalize and understand those rules. This is the function of Binah. Think of Binah as the head coach of a national team. This figure understands the rules, possesses knowledge of the game, maintains direct contact with the club's management, and is responsible for the players. Binah ensures the well-being of the players and pushes them to improve, just as a mother would with her children. The head coach does not participate in the field; he directs from the sidelines.

By now, you can probably see the broader analogy with soccer. **The Stadium** represents **the World**, while **the Field** represents your **Mind** and **Emotions,** —where you experience all possibilities. The **Game** itself represents your **Life**, where the manifestation of every decision you make is experienced. Goals aren't scored from outside the field -manifestation occurs only within the game.

During the game, our attention is on **the Ball**, it symbolizes the **Present Moment**, where soccer is experienced with all its intensity. The ball has no preferences. It doesn't root for any team; it is not in a hurry for the game to end, nor does it need goals to be scored. Life is like that—it simply IS. It unfolds solely in the only moment we experience life - the present moment.

Let's understand the soccer field as the place where you choose to experience YOUR OWN LIFE—not anyone else's. That's why you will never hear a coach say, "This corner kick is too difficult for you; let me take it." We came into the world to test ourselves, to feel, to play, to experience, and to take responsibility for our journey. More things are happening off the field than on it. From outside the field, you receive guidance; sometimes, you listen, and other times, not so much.

Occasionally, you can feel your team's crowd supporting you or hear the opposing team's fans trying to distract you from your goal. Both—your supporters and your opponents—push you to become the best version of yourself. Everything conspires in your favor to help you achieve your goal. However, your attention must remain on the game (your life), and you must focus on what is happening on the field (your mind). Anything else distracts you from fulfilling your Tikkun, the spiritual correction process necessary to achieve your purpose.

Similarly, the Sefirot are beyond the perception of your five senses. They serve as your guide; they grant you balance and direction. They help you hold the position you are meant to have in the game of life, ensuring that each movement is in harmony with your divine purpose. However, they will not do the work for you. If you wish to reach a goal—score, defend the ball, or close down the striker before they shoot—you must strive to achieve it. At the end of the match, any additional effort will have no value. What matters is the effort and intention you put into the minutes you played.

When the game ends, you'll meet with your coach, who will review your performance and prepare you for the next challenge. To have the chance to play again, you would have to be reborn. That is why it is crucial to make the most of every minute you have on the field, whether it's 10, 36, 42, 72, 91, or 120.

Some players play on the field the entire match. Others play only half of the game, and some only a few minutes. We can never predict how much time we'll have on the field, so we must not waste the opportunity to play. There are players who step in just five minutes and score the winning goal. That may be their whole purpose.

Returning to Kabbalistic terminology, we have just been introduced to *Arich Anpin*, the name given to the first three Sefirot that transcend the perceptible playing field. This initial block, composed of Keter, Chochmah, and Binah, represents the game itself, with all its rules guided by its head coach and existing at a level of pure potentiality. Although these Sefirot exert a powerful influence on the dynamics of the field, their effects remain undetected by human senses. These higher Sefirot exist in a state of pure potentiality, governing and guiding from an elevated plane, establishing the framework within which all action unfolds.

Chochmah and Binah represent the archetypal father and mother. Binah receives from Chochmah and longs to share that abundance. For Binah to nurture, it requires a vessel—something capable of receiving from her. From this dynamic, the next phase of desire emerges: a level created specifically to receive that flow of abundance.

This divine union gives rise to the next set of six Sefirot, collectively known as *Zeir Anpin*, or "Small Face." These emotional attributes reflect the practical dimensions of life where divine potential is realized in action.

The Tree of Life with the six Sefirot of *Zeir Anpin* in black

ZEIR ANPIN

Zeir Anpin consists of the six emotional attributes: Chesed, Gevurah, Tiferet, Netzach, Hod, and Yesod. It represents a level of divine manifestation that must be integrated and work in unity to reflect the perfect balance of the universe. Each of these Sefirot not only possesses its own name and energy but also symbolizes a specific characteristic that influences our daily lives and behavior.

We can view *Zeir Anpin* as the players on the team who face challenges and are aware of their responsibility on the field.

Although human experience is unique to each individual, it reaches its full potential when working as a team. No one makes significant progress or scores goals in life by running across the entire field alone. When we support each other, we become a team instead of just isolated players. This is the role of *Zeir Anpin*: to support us on our journey.

The six Sefirot of *Zeir Anpin* represent attributes that we must correct and balance. These Sefirot do not function in isolation; rather, they are interconnected and must operate in harmony to reflect spiritual balance and wholeness. By correcting and harmonizing these qualities, we can achieve a state of internal equilibrium that manifests in our actions and relationships with others, thus contributing to a more orderly and harmonious universe.

The Sefirot have specific locations in the human body, as illustrated below:

- **Chesed**: Right arm symbolizes kindness and expansion.

- **Gevurah**: Left arm represents strength and restraint.

- **Tiferet**: Torso balances and harmonizes the energies of Chesed and Gevurah.

- **Netzach**: Right leg symbolizes perseverance and victory.

- **Hod**: Left leg embodies humility and gratitude.

- **Yesod**: Reproductive organs, connect all the other Sefirot.

At the same time, since they are the foundation of all existence, we can also represent them in the context of soccer to better illustrate how they act and what energies they channel:

- **Chesed**: The generous player who passes the ball and supports his teammates.

- **Gevurah**: The strong defender who ensures the team's defense.

- **Tiferet**: The midfielder who balances attack and defense.

- **Netzach**: The unstoppable and persevering player.

- **Hod**: The strategist who has a deep connection with the game and inspires their teammates.

- **Yesod**: The captain who connects all the players and ensures the team functions as a unit.

By understanding the Sefirot in the context of the human body and soccer, we visualize how these qualities and attributes must work together to achieve balance and harmony, both in the spiritual realm and in practical life.

CHESED

Chesed, the fourth Sefirah in the Tree of Life, counting from Keter, is translated from Hebrew as 'mercy.' It represents the qualities of the desire to give, kindness, and sharing.

Chesed is associated with positive polarity and, in the human body, with the right arm, nails, and semen. Nails have the ability to regenerate when cut, and semen is an essential source of life. Similarly, milk reflects Chesed's essence, transforming into cream, butter, or cheese during preservation, endlessly offering its derivatives. All these elements share the color white, symbolizing Chesed's ability to reflect all the light it receives, radiating purity and abundance.

In nature, Chesed is compared to water, which flows freely into any space where it is allowed to enter, being a source of life. Just as water sustains the earth, Chesed sustains the world through acts of generosity.

There is no movement without desire. Just as a primordial desire gave rise to the creation of this world, every action stems from an initial impulse that propels it forward. Similarly, a soccer game begins with a pass to a teammate. By initiating the game with this pass, the energy of Chesed is activated, sharing the ball with fellow players and setting the field in motion. Holding onto the ball and advancing individually across the field generates a rush of adrenaline—a surge of excitement that fuels the player. Yet, clinging to that adrenaline for too long will exhaust even the most skilled athlete. Players must constantly make passes and execute plays, weaving a collective rhythm that drives the game forward. This is how soccer is played, and it is how we advance in the game of life.

Chesed is the first action that, when originating from a pure level of consciousness, manifests with that same purity in everything that derives from that action. Chesed is the way light manifests in this world, pure and simple.

To give, it is essential first to have something to offer. In Kabbalah, the importance of cultivating within ourselves that which we wish to share is emphasized, allowing us to become a source of abundance. Sharing connects us to a greater purpose, generating a flow of energy and fostering our personal growth.

This principle applies both to the material—such as sharing money with someone in need or half of our lunch to a friend—and to the spiritual, by giving love, acting with patience, sharing a smile, or offering advice. Sharing from the heart connects us with a greater purpose, we not only meet an external need but also find fulfillment, purpose, and personal growth.

Giving implies action and requires effort, yet this does not mean Chesed is associated with pain or suffering. When

Chesed is expressed at an elevated level, it entails genuine giving without expecting anything in return. However, when the energy of Chesed has yet to be refined in us, the act of giving can become distorted. For example, it may paradoxically lead to selfishness (giving in order to receive), recklessness (giving to the point of losing everything), adopting a victim mentality to gain recognition for having given, or giving out of obligation. Likewise, excessive sharing without balance can lead to exploitation. In all these cases, the imbalance reflects a difficulty in managing the quality of Chesed. These ways of acting do not lead to true fulfillment.

The Bible tells us the story of the patriarch Abraham*, who embodies the quality of Chesed in this world. Abraham kept his tent open in all directions to welcome and care for travelers passing by. God changed his name from Abram to Abraham, adding the Hebrew letter hei (ה) to reflect the achievement he reached by becoming the channel of Chesed in the world. This name change was not the cause but rather the result of his spiritual work.

With this modification, the numerology of his name in Hebrew came to sum 248[2], related to the parts of the body and the number of words in the *Shema Yisrael**, a central declaration of faith in Judaism. This connection suggests the importance of giving with our entire being, in a loving and selfless way.

The principle of sharing and teamwork is not only a characteristic of soccer but also reflects a fundamental principle in the creation of the world, manifested and evident in the very gift of life itself. The *Zohar* teaches that the world was created with an immense desire to share. This idea is clearly manifested in the Sefirah of Chesed, which symbolizes kindness and unconditional love. The essence of the Creator's light is to give and share without expecting anything in return. When we act in a manner similar to the light, selflessly sharing with others, we align ourselves with our true spiritual essence.

Let's examine the phrase from Genesis 2:4: "These are the generations of the heavens and the earth when they **were created**." At first glance, the term **"were created"** (in Hebrew, *behibaram*) might seem redundant and unnecessary. However, in Hebrew, ***behibaram*** (בְּהִבָּרְאָם) contains the same letters as as "***be-Abraham***" (בְּאַבְרָהָם), which translates as "by Abraham." This suggests that the world was created with the energy of Chesed that Abraham personifies, a force of selfless giving that binds creation together.

[2]In the Hebrew alphabet, each letter has a numerical value. Abraham's original name was Abram (אברם), with the numerical values Aleph (א) = 1, Bet (ב) = 2, Resh (ר) = 200, and Mem (ם) = 40, totaling 243. When God changed his name to Abraham (אברהם), the letter Hei (ה) with a value of 5 was added, making the values Aleph (א) = 1, Bet (ב) = 2, Resh (ר) = 200, Hei (ה) = 5, and Mem (ם) = 40, totaling 248. Therefore, the numerology of Abraham (אברהם) sums to 248.

The *Zohar* explains that this energy of selfless sharing is essential for the world's existence; without it, the world could not sustain itself even for an instant. Abraham's kindness and unconditional love not only represent human virtues but also reflect the divine essence that sustains the universe.

We have seen how limitless sharing represents an unbalanced Chesed, which can lead to an excess of generosity. Therefore, from Chesed emerges the next Sefirah: Gevurah.

GEVURAH

The fifth Sefirah is called Gevurah, translated from Hebrew as "strength" or "judgment." It represents the qualities of severity and discipline. Gevurah is associated with negative polarity and corresponds to the left arm of the human body. It symbolizes the second day of creation, when the first separation from infinite unity emerges. Gevurah is understood as the force that restricts and limits the overflowing expansion of Chesed, ensuring that it is channeled appropriately so that the game does not descend into chaos. For instance, without the presence of Gevurah, the grass would never stop growing, as the expansive energy of Chesed would simply have no restraint.

Imagine you are in a soccer game where each player and movement can be perceived through the principles of Chesed and Gevurah. In this case, Chesed manifests as the generous act of passing the ball among players. However, for a team to be successful, it cannot rely solely on Chesed. This is where Gevurah comes in, representing the discipline and restraint necessary to structure the game and maintain its purpose.

Gevurah embodies judgment, an action needed for

tough decisions on the field, such as committing a strategic foul to prevent a goal or contending with opponents to gain control of the ball. Gevurah also manifests in defense, setting limits on the opposing team and guarding one's goal. It is the force that channels discipline with intention, ensuring precise restraint to prevent chaos and guide players toward growth through challenges.

Without the presence of an opponent on the field, there is no possibility for growth, nor can the game truly unfold as a transformative experience. Challenge and competition are essential for the ongoing development and improvement of both the team and the players. Gevurah provides the strength to overcome these obstacles, transforming resistance into opportunities for refinement.

When Gevurah is out of balance, it can lead to overly strict enforcement of rules, ignoring the spirit of the game. This imbalance manifests as harsh judgment on every play and excessive discipline, creating an unbearable playing environment that stifles the enjoyment of the sport. Similarly, an unbalanced Gevurah energy generates a rigid life experience, filled with constant criticism, devoid of grace, and difficult to endure. It becomes a force that constricts rather than constructs, blocking the flow of Divine Light.

To illustrate the potential of Gevurah, consider this example. Imagine a thief who, with cold intent, uses a knife to harm a person to steal what does not belong to him. In this situation, the thief channels Gevurah's energy negatively, focusing solely on fulfilling his selfish desire, without empathy for the victim. Now, imagine a surgeon using a scalpel to save a life. In both cases, these two individuals are drawing on Gevurah's energy to make an incision in another's body. If we focus only on the physical actions, then both appear identical, as they involve cutting someone's skin. However, the 1% of physical reality lacks meaning on its own; it is the consciousness and intention behind our actions that give them true purpose. The essence of each act lies in its intention, not mere physical execution. The thief uses Gevurah destructively and selfishly, while the surgeon channels it constructively and altruistically. This distinction reveals how the same energy can be channeled differently depending on the intention that directs it.

Some people simplify their understanding by considering Chesed as something good and Gevurah as something bad. But this is a superficial perception, far from the truth. Good and bad are human constructs based on limited comparisons—they are not inherent qualities of the divine energies that govern the world. In Kabbalah, Chesed and Gevurah are complementary forces, both essential for the harmony of creation.

Gevurah is represented in the Torah by the patriarch Isaac*, whose name in Hebrew translates as "laughter." According to the *Zohar*, laughter gives us the ability to view moments of difficulty with grace. When we are able to laugh at ourselves, challenging situations become more bearable.

Isaac also shows us an incredible willingness to follow orders. This is evident in the Torah story known as the Binding of Isaac, when he is taken by his father, Abraham, to Mount Moriah. With great determination and in obedience to God's command, Abraham prepares his son for what seemed to be his sacrifice. However, at the last moment, an angel stops Abraham's hand, revealing God's true intention. In this narrative, Isaac represents the desire to receive, channeling the energy of Gevurah, while Abraham symbolizes the desire to share, channeling the energy of Chesed.

This story teaches us that our desire to receive must be bound to serve the desire to share. This principle is reflected in Judaism, for example, in the daily practice of wearing *Tefillin**—phylacteries, which contain sacred scriptures that are placed on the head, bound to the arm, and positioned near the heart. This act balances the energies of Chesed and Gevurah within us. By binding the arm (representing the desire to receive) and directing it toward sharing through our thoughts and desires (head and heart), we harmonize these forces, aligning our actions with divine purpose.

The essence of the Torah lies in understanding its teachings beyond their literal meaning. This is affirmed by Rabbi Shimon Bar Yochai that declares: "*Woe to those who say that the Torah came only to relate simple stories!*" (*Zohar* Vol. 3, 152a). The *Zohar* teaches that every word of the Torah carries a hidden meaning, and those who only see the surface-level stories do not truly comprehend its significance (paraphrased from *Zohar*

Vol. 1, 47b). In reality, these stories are garments that conceal deeper and mystical truths.

In summary, both in life and in soccer, Chesed promotes collaboration, while Gevurah ensures structured progress. However, this is not enough to guarantee success on the field. Let's keep moving forward...

THE OPPOSING TEAM

The Creator instilled desire in each one of us. Without desire, nothing would manifest in the physical realm. This desire is, in fact, an ancestral connection we share with infinite fulfillment—a state of completeness we once experienced and now yearn to reclaim. Therefore, desire is not inherently negative; rather, it is a powerful force that can be fulfilled in two ways. When our desire aligns and resonates with divine harmony, it draws us closer to true fulfillment. However, when this desire is directed solely toward personal gratification, it distances us from the Divine Light we long to experience.

In Hebrew, the word for "evil" is ***Ra*** (רַע). It is an acronym for ***R****atzon* ***A****tzmi*, which translates as “a desire for oneself.” According to Kabbalah, evil is not an independent force but a misdirected desire, one that is focused on selfish receiving. It is a distortion of the original desire for infinite sharing, which chose to contract itself to descend into this physical world, thus setting the stage for the game of life.

The objective of the game we're playing is to transform our selfish desire (*Ratzon Atzmi*) to fulfill our needs into *Ratzon LeAshpia**—a desire to receive in order to share, to positively influence others, to live with purpose, to engage with those around us, and to merit Divine Light.

In Kabbalah, the opposing team is known as *Yetzer Hara**. This term refers to the inclination toward evil or the negative impulse present in every individual. In truth, this impulse is life's way of directing our focus where it is needed the most. By presenting challenges that push us to grow, improve, and rectify our actions. We recognize the *Yetzer Hara* when we feel the urge to act selfishly, disregarding others. When we blame the opposing team for our struggles and avoid taking responsibility for what happens in our lives. However, this "opposing team" is a blessing, essential for revealing abilities we would otherwise never discover. It drives us to face and overcome challenges that, without its presence, we might not even recognize or be able to conquer.

Let's look at the *Yetzer Hara* in action with this example: In the 2006 FIFA World Cup final between France and Italy, French player Zinedine Zidane scored a penalty goal just seven minutes into the game. Only five minutes later, Italy equalized thanks to Marco Materazzi, keeping the score tied 1-1 for the remainder of the match. In extra time, at the 110th minute, after an exchange of insults with Materazzi, Zidane headbutted the Italian player in the chest, knocking him to the ground and receiving a red card.

This incident vividly illustrates the *Yetzer Hara* in action: with just a single thought planted in Zidane's mind, it triggered a surge of emotions that led to an impulsive act. This momentary lapse not only affected Zidane but also harmed his team, contributing to their defeat in the penalty shootout that followed. Although Zidane won the tournament's Golden Ball, his expulsion prevented him from collecting his award or runner-up medal.

The exact words exchanged with Materazzi are irrelevant; we are not taking sides in this situation. This is an example from which we can draw a lesson for our lives. I chose this story among many in soccer because it shows that there are second chances. Zidane could have remained trapped in that incident and gone down in history for his infamous headbutt, instead, he overcame that moment. He is now recognized not only as one of soccer's most iconic players, but also for the three Champions League titles he has won as a coach.

Modern soccer, as we know it today, originated in 19th-century England. This may be one of the reasons the Zohar does not use it as an example in its teachings. Kabbalists drew upon the stories and contexts of their own time; nevertheless, we can learn a great deal from them.

For example, the *Zohar* (2:163a) explains the nature of the inclination toward evil through a parable: It resembles a king who wishes to prove whether his son is ready to become a leader. As a test, he hires a prostitute to tempt his son in various ways. Yet, the son does not succumb to her temptation and grows stronger through adversity. It becomes clear that the king's son is ready for the next level of leadership. However, who enabled the son to overcome and demonstrate his abilities to the king? The prostitute. So, was she bad or good? She serves as a means by which Light is revealed in the world, earned through worthiness.

The Zohar teaches that the *Yetzer Hara* originally existed as an external force—distant and recognizable. With the creation of the world and our choice to descend into this plane to participate in the game of life, this force was integrated into us, becoming an inner adversary. Within every human being, the *Yetzer Hara* works subtly, planting thoughts and ideas and gradually taking control of our minds when we give it room to act. This deceptive 'enemy' does not present itself as an external threat but instead adopts the voice of our very self, disguising itself as us. Recognizing it becomes the ultimate challenge, and the key to winning this game lies in consciousness: only by becoming aware of its influence can we begin to free ourselves from its influence.

The *Yetzer Hara* aims to make you analyze and rationalize situations to justify them. It is as sly as you are and will speak to you in ways that capture your attention. It wields all the tools necessary to perform its job and does it perfectly. Paradoxically, it desires to be defeated, as it, too, is part of the game of life.

If you choose to believe the thoughts implanted by the Yetzer Hara, you will think you are right. And if you think you are right, guess what? You will be. Remember: you are the director of the movie of your life—and with it, the reality you experience.

The *Yetzer Hara* resides quietly yet persistently in our minds. When we make space for it, it uses every trick to create, like an illusionist, uncomfortable or painful scenarios in our lives. These situations are designed to catch our attention and lead us to do the inner work we are meant to do. However, as difficult as it may be to understand, the suffering born from these situations does not come from the *Yetzer Hara* but from our distancing ourselves from The Light.

The stories we tell ourselves may help justify our suffering, but they will not allow us to grow. The situation, whatever it may be, that prevented you from scoring a goal in your life is not really important. That is simply part of the world's illusion, designed to distract you. The key lies in understanding "for what purpose" rather than "why" we experience a situation in a particular way. Becoming aware of this disrupts the narrative pattern within our minds and allows us, in that moment, to exercise free will and alter our thoughts. Remember, every situation in life carries a lesson, guiding us toward transformation.

In Kabbalah, pain is seen as a point—an inevitable, momentary signal calling our attention to something that needs to be addressed. Suffering, however, is a line, a continuous sequence of unresolved moments (dots) of pain that we prolong. While pain is inevitable, suffering is optional. Pain itself is not the problem; rather, our resistance to experiencing and addressing it in a timely manner transforms it into suffering.

The interpretation we give to what happens is what shapes our reality. Experiences take place within us; they are not external. We alone assign meaning to what occurs to us. No external event holds the power to dictate how we experience it.

I am fully aware of how easy it is to write these ideas compared to the challenge of facing and overcoming our *Yetzer Hara*. It is like watching a soccer match and wishing to instruct a player on what to do, judging comfortably from our sofa, wearing socks, far from the field's intensity. These teachings aim to inspire us to do our own inner work, rather than focusing on the shortcomings of others.

THE KLIPOT

Klipot (singular: *Klipa**) literally translates from Hebrew as "shells" or "husks." In Kabbalah, they represent metaphysical barriers that conceal the Divine Light, preventing its complete manifestation in the physical world. These shells are formed through our negative actions; they act as obstacles that separate us from the Creator's Light, limiting our access to the blessings destined for us.

Rav Ashlag, in his work *Talmud Eser Sefirot*, explains that the *Klipot* correspond to a precise measure of our uncorrected egoistic desire. The more selfish our desire is, the stronger the barrier we must overcome. The *Klipot* act as forces that conceal the Divine Light and drive us away from it.

Light is the one true existence—it IS existence itself. Therefore, we cannot truly distance ourselves from it. We either manifest it in our lives or surrender it to the *Klipa*, creating a temporary illusion in which we no longer perceive The Light's presence in our lives.

Consider this example that illustrates how the *Klipot* function. Imagine a lamp in a room, its light obscured by several layers of clothing that you have placed over it. The light from the lamp continues to shine, but the layers prevent it from being perceived in the room.

Now, let us draw an analogy: color is a phenomenon created by the projection of light, while black represents the absence of light, meaning that, in truth, black is not a color. Paradoxically, this does not prevent us from experiencing it as one in daily life. According to Kabbalistic teachings, black is filled with Light that has been absorbed (pure desire to receive for oneself) and is therefore "trapped" by the *Klipa*. In Kabbalah, black represents Light in a state where its radiance can no longer be perceived.

When you turn off the light

in a room, where does the light go?

Nowhere—it remains present

in an unrevealed state.

TIFERET

In Kabbalah, Tiferet is most often translated as "beauty," and it signifies the harmony that arises when opposing forces are balanced. It is the integration point between Chesed (loving-kindness) and Gevurah (judgment-discipline)—two energies that, when unified through Tiferet, enable the Divine Light to flow in a balanced and constructive way. Positioned along the central column of the Tree of Life, Tiferet mediates between the expansive generosity of Chesed and the necessary restraint of Gevurah. When these three Sefirot are aligned, they create a balance, reflecting the beauty and perfection that emerge from this union.

Within the spiritual realm, Tiferet represents acting with the qualities of the Infinite Light maintaining balance and integrating all the forces of the universe in harmony. Our connection with Tiferet allows us to vibrate with the same frequency of the Light and, through affinity of form, to receive its radiance in a state of harmonious flow.

On the soccer field, Tiferet reveals itself in a well-executed sequence of passes that culminate in a goal. The harmony of coordinated teamwork on the field reflects the beauty of Tiferet. Perhaps this is where the phrase "what a beautiful goal" comes from. True beauty resides in balance, both in spiritual life and the material world.

The physical world is sustained by perfect balance, based on atoms—the fundamental elements that make up all matter. Atoms combine with one another to create everything we know in the physical world. If we examine the structure of an atom, we see that it is composed of protons, electrons, and neutrons. In Kabbalah, these components correspond to the principles of Chesed (protons), Gevurah (electrons), and Tiferet (neutrons). These subatomic particles exist primarily within a seemingly empty space. However, it is precisely this empty space that allows for the manifestation of matter and the illusion of our physical world.

The proton has a positive charge that attracts the electron, which resides in an orbital around the atom's nucleus. The neutron stabilizes the nucleus by counteracting the repulsion between protons. This balance between positive and negative charges, along with the stabilization of the nucleus, is what sustains the existence of matter. This example of the subatomic world illustrates how science and Kabbalah communicate fundamental concepts in their respective languages, revealing the connection between the physical and spiritual worlds.

Let's analyze the function of a conventional light bulb from the perspective of the Sefirot. We find a positive pole representing Chesed, which activates and directs energy. On the other hand, the negative pole receives that energy, symbolizing Gevurah. Between these two poles lies the filament's resistance, identified with Tiferet. It regulates the flow of energy, prevents a short circuit, and enables the steady, enduring emission of light.

Without this resistance, a direct union between opposite poles would produce a sudden intense but ephemeral flash of light. Resistance, represented by Tiferet, balances these opposing forces, producing a stable and continuous light. This balance illustrates how the principle of the Sefirot manifests in all aspects of creation, integrating and harmonizing the forces of expansion and restriction. Tiferet allows us to reveal a constant and lasting light in our lives.

In life, the Light you need is already within you—always present, accompanying you in exactly the measure you require. It is the act of resistance, whether you apply it or avoid it, that determines how much Light you will reveal in your life. Resistance not only balances and harmonizes the forces of Chesed and Gevurah, but also allows us to experience the Light in a continuous and sustained way, thereby revealing our true essence and spiritual potential.

Tiferet is essential for attaining balance. Without its presence, any action would lack harmony. While you might be able to generate fleeting sparks of light, it would not be possible to manifest a steady, enduring light. Only by integrating this balance can we achieve a continuous flow of light that leads us to a state of lasting fulfillment. Kabbalah, through its teachings, guides us toward this balance.

In the human body, two vital organs, the heart and the lungs, exemplify this essential equilibrium. The heart pumps blood in a balanced act of giving and receiving—essential for life. If the heart were to possess its own consciousness and ego and attempt to hoard blood, out of fear of losing it, it would ultimately cause its own demise. Similarly, the lungs sustain life by inhaling and exhaling air. Imagining a lung holding on to air out of fear of releasing it may sound absurd, yet it reminds us of how selfish human behaviors often contradict the vital balance required for life. Can you imagine a tree trying to absorb all the water from the earth before the tree next to it does, thinking it might never rain again? That pattern of thinking is one we repeat daily, creating an imbalance we could avoid if we flowed with a conscious balance.

Life manifests in the harmony between receiving and sharing—a fundamental principle in both human anatomy and Kabbalah.

Illustration of the Tree of Life overlaid with the distribution of players on the field.

As shown in the graphic, soccer players advance through triangular passing sequences. This interaction is one of the most effective ways to play, creating patterns that mirror the structure of the Tree of Life. True stars don't play solo; they work together and pass the ball to each other.

Soccer players can push forward and try to score goals on their own, but the true stars of soccer—those who deeply understand the game—move forward by relying on their teammates, creating harmony on the field. When that harmony is lost, so is the ball, and getting it back requires hard work. Life follows a similar pattern: when we make mistakes, we must try again to restore balance. Reaching this harmony is not easy, and recovering the ball can be even more challenging. Therefore, it is essential to choose your battles with wisdom and discernment.

Life constantly presents us with challenges and opportunities to learn and grow. Just like in soccer, where coordination and teamwork are crucial for success, in life we must work in harmony with others and our environment. True fulfillment is achieved when we find and maintain this balance, allowing the Infinite Light of the Creator to manifest through our actions and relationships.

At the origin of the thought of creation, at the level of Keter, perfect harmony was always present. However, in the realm of human experience, this balance appears distorted so that we can take part in the game of life. In every game, as in life itself, laws and rules were conceived to create conditions that allow for an environment where the game can unfold—providing us with the experiences we need and promoting our growth and learning.

The world, in its essence, always maintains its balance, even if our limited mind cannot always see or comprehend it. Our challenge lies in discovering inner balance so that we can then experience that same harmony in our daily lives.

Achieving this inner balance is not an easy task, yet it is essential for attaining fulfillment and true peace. Life constantly invites us to find a state of alignment. But balance is not static—just like in a game, where you can't hold the ball for too long. You must keep moving, passing it from side to side, pursuing harmony in every moment, in every play. Such is life itself.

In the Bible, Tiferet is symbolized by the patriarch Jacob*, who lived a life marked by continuous effort and trials, overcoming obstacles along his path. In a pivotal moment in his life, Jacob confronts an angel who embodies his greatest adversity. Despite this, Jacob defeats him in battle and emerges victorious. As a recognition of his triumph, the angel—whom the *Zohar* refers to as *Satan**—blesses him with a new name: Israel.

In Hebrew, *Satan* (שטן) signifies "to oppose" or "adversary." From this perspective, Satan represents the challenges and trials a person faces on their path of spiritual ascension.

The letters of the name **Jacob** (יעקב) in Hebrew **sum to 182.** The letters of the name **Satan** (שטן) in Hebrew **sum to 359. 182 + 359 = 541**.

Why is this numerology relevant?

This story holds profound symbolism: Jacob confronts and triumphs over his most formidable opponent—an angel who had been guarding a light destined for him, awaiting Jacob's victory in order to release it. By overcoming his adversary, Jacob symbolically adds the angel's numerical value (called Satan) to his own and receives the new name: Israel.

Guess what? The numerical value in Hebrew of **Israel equals 541**.

The word *Israel* in Hebrew is composed of two words (ישר-אל): *Yashar*, meaning to go forward in a direct way, and *El*, alluding to God. As the name suggests, Israel (straight to God) represents those individuals whose main objective in the game of life is to attain a higher state of consciousness, developing an affinity with the Creator.

This task is accomplished through the consistent, daily effort to overcome our opponent, defeat our selfish nature, and thus remove the veils that block the Divine Light in our lives. This name symbolizes a steady spiritual ascent—an invitation to face both internal and external challenges with integrity and purpose, always striving for connection with the divine.

In soccer, overcoming obstacles involves breaking past the defense's mark, orchestrating a strategic play, resisting provocations from the opposing team, dribbling through the defense, successfully shooting at the goal, and finally scoring a goal. If you manage to do this consistently, your efforts will transform into medals, trophies, winning championships, and even a spot in the World Cup. These achievements bring joy not only to you but to your entire team, your family, your fans, and your nation. Overcoming challenges generates blessings that ripple far beyond individual success.

There is a story in the Torah in which Jacob prepares a red lentils stew, and his brother Esau*, hungry, desires it so intensely that he agrees to sell his birthright for a bowl. Taken literally, the story may seem senseless. That is the reason we must not interpret it literally. Instead, I invite you to view it through the lens of Kabbalah, a different perspective that allows us to perceive a deeper meaning.

Esau represents impulsive actions, our pursuit of instant gratification without regard for long-term consequences. This is not merely a material transaction, but rather a depiction of the struggle between short-term desire (Esau) and higher spiritual purpose (Jacob). The birthright symbolizes our connection to the divine, and the true challenge lies in resisting fleeting rewards in order to remain aligned with our higher selves.

Just like the player who commits a reckless foul for a quick gain and earns a red card, Esau gives up his eternal spiritual inheritance for a short-term, temporary physical pleasure. Kabbalah teaches that the true test lies in the ability to master the ego, training ourselves to delay immediate gratification so we can attain lasting fulfillment.

In conclusion, the harmony we find in Tiferet is reflected in our daily lives. Striving to achieve this balance is not just a spiritual concept—it is a reality that manifests in all aspects of life, from science to sports.

DIRECT LIGHT vs. INDIRECT LIGHT

Kabbalah refers to direct light, *Or Yashar**, as The Light that is received without obstacles, straight from the Source, without having earned it or being prepared to handle it. Because we have not earned it, we cannot retain it. This Light fulfills our desires with intensity-but only temporarily. It burns us and does not remain with us. It is a flash of intense radiance that does not endure.

The Light we truly seek is the indirect light, *Or Chozer**, which arises from the effort to share. This is the true, eternal light that brings blessings into our lives. We then discover that the greatest light of all may be available to us, but only if we have earned the right to receive it. How do we do that? By transforming our Desire to Receive for oneself into a Desire to Share. That is the power of Tiferet. This principle is ever-present and serves as the foundation of all the Mitzvot (spiritual connections practiced in Judaism).

The Hebrew calendar is based primarily on the moon, whose light we perceive indirectly, since the moon does not emit its own light but reflects that of the sun. The sun emits a much greater light, which reaches us directly; yet, because of its intensity, it burns us and we cannot look at it directly. Judaism uses the lunar calendar because the light we seek must also be indirect—resulting from an act of sharing. Similarly, the *kippah**, a head covering that restricts the direct light we receive, allows us to connect indirectly with the Divine Light of the Creator.

Receiving direct light can be very pleasurable, but since it is a fleeting light that does not remain with us, it leads us to need more and more in order to feel satisfied. No matter how much you receive, if it comes from the ego and is drawn directly, that sensation will be temporary and will inevitably return you to the initial lack that gave rise to that original desire.

A #lifehack you can start applying right away is to ask yourself before taking any action: When will I be receiving the Light resulting from this action?

For example, before starting a soccer training session, you might feel too lazy to get out of bed and head to the field. In this case, the true Light is felt once you overcome the laziness, complete your training, and end up feeling amazing. This is because the Light is received as a consequence of effort.

Now imagine sneaking into a soccer stadium without paying, slipping in quietly among the crowd. In that moment, you might feel a rush of adrenaline. However, by trying to take that Light directly and without having earned it, you create a veil (*Klipa*) with that action—one that distances you from the Light. The rules of the game have already accounted for every possibility from the beginning and include numerous mechanisms to balance the scales. In truth, there is no way to cheat the system through actions that connect you to direct light.

Consider another example: enjoying a piece of chocolate cake (assuming you love it as much as I do) becomes direct Light (*Or Yashar*) when you eat it in excess. After the first bite, you've already experienced its flavor, and each additional bite provides the same sensation as the one before. So how much pleasure then, do you need before it becomes overwhelming and becomes too much?

We can go even further—if you overeat, you judge yourself and feel bad. That experience doesn't serve you much. And yet, it's precisely that last piece of cake—the one you shouldn't have eaten—that teaches you a valuable lesson. If you learn from the experience in that moment, you can even be grateful for that final spoonful. It's precisely that last bite that helps you recognize your limits and understand that you shouldn't repeat the excess.

Now that we've understood the importance of incorporating Divine Light into our daily actions in an indirect way, and how our actions and desires influence how we receive the Divine Light, let's now explore another fundamental concept before continuing with the Sefirot: free will.

FREE WILL

Have you ever considered how many decisions you make in a single day, not just significant decisions, but even seemingly minor ones, like asking your body to move a foot? Studies suggest that an average person makes around 35,000 choices daily. Many of these are trivial, such as choosing which shoes to wear or deciding whether to start walking with your right or left foot. Even seemingly automatic actions—like unlacing a shoe before putting it on or forcing your foot into it—are choices. Some decisions carry more weight: Should I go out or stay home? Should I continue in my current job or pursue a different path? Should I pass the ball or shoot toward the goal? Even the simple act of reading these lines could be interpreted either as an act of free will or as something predetermined, destined to occur. As your day progresses, you still have about 34,995 decisions left to make. However, are we truly free to make these choices?

Let us examine this through the lens of Kabbalah. Imagine watching a recorded soccer match, already knowing the final score. The experience would likely feel dull, failing to spark excitement or hold your attention, as the outcome is predetermined. Similarly, life gains meaning when the future is uncertain, and multiple paths lie before us.

Without options, we become enslaved by the circumstances that surround us. A slave is someone who merely follows orders, deprived of the freedom to choose or make independent decisions. We can remain in such a state unknowingly, drifting through an entire lifetime without ever realizing our bondage. The greatest achievement of the *Yetzer Hara* is keeping us enslaved throughout our lives, all while convincing us that we are free simply because we pursue our selfish desires when, in truth, we are serving our egoistic instincts. It dictates which desires to fulfill at any given moment, shapes our thoughts, and traps us in a web of fleeting emotions. The real game of life begins only when we become aware that we have options and start making conscious decisions. Even the choice to refrain from choosing is, in itself, a decision.

When we allow ourselves to be ruled by our selfish desires, we lose our true freedom. In satisfying the ego, we are actually feeding a cunning inner master—one that knows our weaknesses and speaks in the language of our most intimate desires and thoughts. We must not underestimate it, as it disguises itself as whatever is necessary to capture our attention. True free will begins the moment we choose to become conscious—when we decide not to be slaves to our own thoughts and emotions. It is this power—the ability to pause, reflect, and respond with intention—that activates our freedom. Only then can we reveal the Light hidden within our existence, rather than remain puppets pulled by the strings of the ego.

Imagine stepping onto a soccer field chewing gum and deciding to throw it onto the grass. Minutes later, you inadvertently step on it and become annoyed, without realizing that you were the one who created that situation. In each play of life, we are consistently presented with the opportunity to avoid the problems we have brought upon ourselves. To achieve this, it is essential to become aware that the "gum on the grass" is our own creation. We can avoid stepping on it if we acknowledge we put it there in the first place.

With every play you make in life, you have the opportunity to choose between being bound by the situation or freeing yourself from it. Only when you are aware of both possibilities can you truly make a choice. The purpose of Kabbalah is to help you become a conscious player.

The balance between the possibility of loss and the opportunity to win is essential for creating a space where free will gives meaning and satisfaction to victory. True free will is not about changing the events that occur, but about how we choose our responses. Although we cannot control external circumstances, we do have the ability to choose how we respond in every situation. This principle implies that each challenge and each success is designed by Divine Providence for our spiritual growth.

"I've missed more than 9,000 shots in my career. I've lost almost 300 games. Twenty-six times, I've been trusted to take the game-winning shot and missed.

I've failed over and over and over again in my life. And that is why I succeed."

Michael Jordan

NETZACH

Netzach, translated as "victory," occupies the seventh position on the Tree of Life, counting from Keter, and is located directly beneath Chesed. It represents the transformation of Chesed's generosity into purposeful action. In the human body, Netzach corresponds to the right leg, paired with Hod (the left leg); together, they enable us to walk the path and act as vessels for applying what we have learned. It is the driving force that propels us forward with determination, embodying a pragmatic consciousness reflected in its association with the right leg, the limb that leads us into motion.

Having understood how to harness Chesed, Gevurah, and Tiferet for teamwork, we now need Netzach's energy to move forward and avoid merely passing the ball back and forth among ourselves. Think of Netzach as a dynamic forward, crossing the midfield line with the ball at your feet, fully in control, ready to break through the opposing team's defenses.

Netzach is represented by Moses*, the leader who guided the Hebrew people to freedom after liberating them from slavery in Egypt. Following the ten plagues, the pivotal moment arrives when Moses stretches out his staff over the Red Sea, which parts, allowing the people of Israel to cross. This story is a powerful metaphor for triumph over our selfish human nature, channeling it to serve our purpose. When you apply this principle in your own life, you free yourself from your ego-driven desires and achieve an inner victory.

The story of Moses in the Torah* represents our consciousness, initially dormant and confined, living within the Pharaoh's palace until it awakens. Only upon realizing that it must break free does the process of spiritual growth begin—one that ultimately leads to liberation from the slavery of ego in Egypt.

In this story, the Egyptians symbolize the opposing team, and while it may appear that they are the ones we must defeat, the true enemy is the *Klipa* we have created within ourselves. Once the *Klipot* are removed, the Divine Light is revealed automatically. Notice that in the narrative, the Jews do not fight the Egyptians; there is no need to battle darkness—what is needed is to allow The Light to be revealed so that the darkness disappears on its own.

In the Torah, the Creator declares to Moses: "Why do you cry out to Me? Tell the Israelites to move forward!" (Exodus 14:15). According to the biblical account, Moses raised his staff and stretched out his hand over the sea, and the waters parted, allowing the Israelites to cross on dry land (Exodus 14:16). However, a complementary rabbinic teaching recounts that Nachshon ben Aminadav*, with unwavering faith, was the first to step into the sea—walking forward until the water reached his neck—before it parted. This act of certainty made it possible for the miracle to manifest.

Crossing the Red Sea symbolizes the inner journey we undertake during adversity to remove the veil of Klipot that prevents us from perceiving the Divine Light. The Light, always present, can finally manifest when we overcome our doubts and act with certainty.

Netzach is associated with the power to overcome obstacles along the path. In addition to being translated as "victory," on a higher level it is also linked to "eternity." Netzach's ultimate triumph will come when, united as humanity, we overcome the *Yetzer Hara* aligned with the eternal flow of Divine Light, attaining spiritual immortality.

Many of the Psalms written by King David* begin with the word *Lamnatzeach*, "To the Conductor," referring to the idea that the Creator orchestrates the world according to a divine plan. The word *Lamnatzeach* shares the root *Netzach*, as it also means "to lead" or "to orchestrate", Reflecting Netzach's role in guiding our actions toward victory.

Netzach and Hod together are like teammates who have crossed the midfield and now face increasing resistance from the opposing team. When Netzach is out of balance, we may believe that victory is solely the result of our individual effort, rather than a collective achievement of the team. In truth, we are only vessels that either allow or block the flow of Divine Light. It is the Creator's Light that flows, reveals, and brings about the accomplishments and right choices that unfold in your life. The moment we attribute our accomplishments to our intelligence, skills, brilliant ideas, or our mental sharpness—or when we compare our victories to those of others or to external measures—we remain in an unrefined state of Netzach.

True victory is achieved over your *Yetzer Hara*. Only then do we reach the ultimate triumph—one that transcends personal ambitions and becomes a collective celebration of Divine Light in action, as we'll explore with Hod's complementary energy.

HOD

Hod, associated with the left leg in the human body, is translated as "glory" and "humility." It is represented by Aaron*, the brother of Moses*, whose humble service as High Priest embodied these virtues. This Sefirah determines when and how you take action in your life.

Hod is the eighth Sefirah, counting from Keter, and its defining virtues are truth and honesty. For this reason, the eighth commandment "You shall not steal," is associated with the qualities of this Sefirah, emphasizing integrity in our actions.

Hod plays a crucial role in managing the driven energies of Netzach. It acts as a vessel of thoughtful restraint, ensuring balance and moderation. When we become overly focused on our goals and desires, Hod reminds us to pause and reassess our actions. It signals when we should shift our intentions, especially if they cloud our connection with others or hinder our spiritual growth.

When refined, Hod allows us to recognize our mistakes, correct them, and move forward. It represents the self-confidence and clarity a soccer player needs to evaluate the situation; in a given moment: to choose to slow down, to pass the ball instead of believing he can advance alone. It embodies the joy of playing in the present moment. We are ignorant in our present, as we have never lived it before. Every play or shot on goal is unique and unrepeatable.

Netzach is that agile and determined player who drives toward the goal, while Hod is the clever, observant, and strategic player. This combination—like a duo on the field—not only allows them to understand the opposing team's movements, but also to anticipate plays before they happen, almost as if they know where the ball is going before anyone kicks it.

The combination of Netzach and Hod allows us to reach a deeper level of the game—beyond the obvious plays—one that can interpret the intention behind each movement. This ability leads us to understand the essence of the plays, like that moment when you sense a goal is about to happen without knowing exactly how; you just know it's coming.

Netzach and Hod are both connected to prophetic capacity, arising from understanding with the heart and acting with honesty, simplicity, and no hidden agendas. It is the player who envisions the ball hitting the net before taking the free kick—not through magic, but by being fully aligned with the flow of the game. These are the moments in life that unfold naturally and cannot be explained, for attempting to analyze them strips away their essence.

An unrefined state of Hod can manifest as a stubbornness that prevents one from admitting mistakes or as a lack of mental flexibility. It is like a player who insists on a failing strategy, refusing to adapt despite the signals and opportunities for change. It is clinging to a single tactic, limiting the potential for growth and the game's evolution. It is obsessing over the how and why of every move, losing the spontaneity and natural flow of play.

When we get stuck in looping thoughts, mental overthinking, or recurring patterns, it prevents us from fully connecting with the game. When we lose our flow—and with it, our connection to the present moment—we struggle to adapt quickly to the new strategies required to keep moving forward. We must be stubborn in our desire to achieve our goals, but not in the methods we use to reach them.

Hod encourages us to prioritize self-care, introspection, and reflection. It emphasizes the importance of slowing down and creating space in our lives to receive divine guidance—like a player pausing to read and understand the field before making a decisive pass.

The true glory of Hod lies in the ability to see beyond our limitations and recognize the Divine Light in all our actions and decisions—to be compassionate and honest.

This understanding allows us to live in harmony with ourselves and with the universe, achieving a balance that reflects the perfection of the Creator, as we now move on to explore the Sefirah of Yesod.

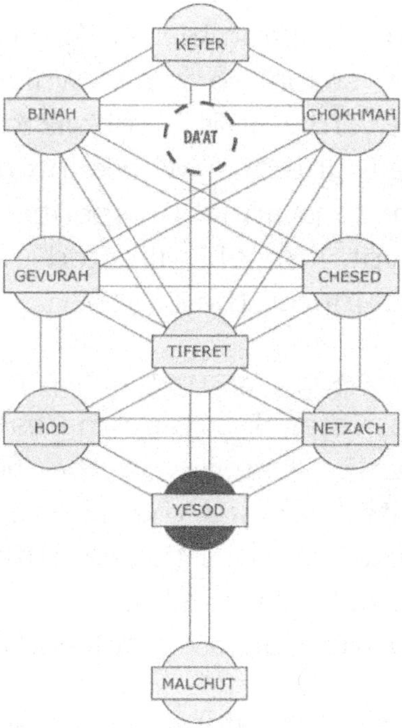

YESOD

Yesod, the ninth Sefirah, means "foundation." We can think of it as a funnel that channels Divine Light from higher levels and helps bring it down into the physical plane. Like a mixer blending sand, water, and cement into solid concrete, Yesod transforms spiritual energy into tangible outcomes.

Yesod serves as the conduit that connects the abstract with the tangible. In the human body, it corresponds to the sexual organs, which manifest inner potential outwardly. It is symbolized by Yosef HaTzadik* (Joseph the Righteous), whose integrity and self-mastery enabled him to channel prosperity. Appointed by the Pharaoh of Egypt, Yosef directed abundance and prosperity throughout the region.

In a soccer team, the captain is the player who leads and motivates his teammates, helping to implement the team's strategy on the field and keeping the group united toward the ultimate goal: scoring. Just as the captain guides the execution of the team's strategy on the field, Yesod channels divine energy, ensuring that the spiritual purpose is fulfilled in tangible reality.

Yesod, like Tiferet, is located along the central axis of the Tree of Life. It acts as a mediator between Netzach and Hod, gathering and condensing the energy that flows from Keter, passing through all the Sefirot until it reaches its final manifestation in the physical realm, in the Sefirah of Malchut. It is comparable to a play in which passes build up and actions accumulate until the opportunity to score a goal finally emerges—thus achieving the objective of the game.

Each individual comes into this world with the purpose of revealing a certain amount of Divine Light. This can be accomplished in two ways: by breaking through the *Klipot* we have created through egoistic actions and by taking actions that manifest Divine Light. In both cases, Yesod plays a crucial role. Here's how.

The *Yetzer Hara* exerts greater pressure as the Light gets closer to manifesting. You can recognize the moments when you are at the level of Yesod by the challenges that arise just before achieving your goals. The greater the Light that is about to be revealed, the stronger the opposition—and the bigger the obstacles you will face.

These difficulties are not accidental; they are designed to strengthen and prepare us. They emerge to provide opportunities to overcome them, grow spiritually, and discover purpose along our path.

The mission of the *Yetzer Hara* is to tempt you to squander opportunities, allowing the *Klipot* to capture the Divine Light. Paradoxically, its true purpose is to be defeated, as it too is part of this game of life. Only when the totality of the Divine Light has been revealed will we collectively emerge victorious.

When the ball is on the opposing team's side of the field, or when their forward is offside, defenders relax their guard. In those moments, there is no real threat of the other team scoring. Similarly, the *Yetzer Hara* doesn't attack until there is a real opportunity to reveal Light. But when a play unfolds and the ball reaches the striker, who is inside the box and about to shoot and score, that's when all kinds of tactics are activated: pushing, kicking, blocks, shouting, and fouls. That exact moment before the shot on goal is what Yesod represents. It illustrates why true opportunities to manifest Light in your life are always preceded by challenges, obstacles, and a tension much like what we feel right before scoring a goal.

In Yesod, there is always opposition, as it is the *Yetzer Hara's* last chance to prevent a positive action from manifesting.

Yesod gathers all the effort we invest—from desire, through thought, and connected to emotion—until it reaches the final outcome, whether it's taking the shot toward the goal or losing the ball to a defender.

Yesod teaches us the importance of being pure channels through which Divine Light can flow in balance and bring blessings into our lives. Through Yesod, abundance reaches this world. Without Yesod, there would be no connection between the celestial and the earthly—it is the conduit that carries divine energy from the higher realms down to Malchut, the next Sefirah we will explore.

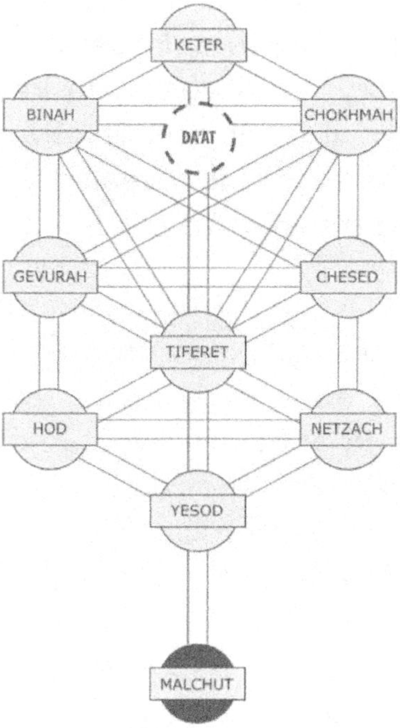

MALCHUT

Malchut is the tenth and final Sefirah in the Tree of Life, translates as "kingdom" and is represented by King David. Unlike the other Sefirot, Malchut possesses no Light of its own—it acts as a vessel to reveal The Light emanating from the higher Sefirot in this physical plane, manifesting what was previously invisible, ethereal, and intangible.

The role of Malchut is essential because it embodies the

point where the abstract becomes concrete. It is the space where spiritual potential transforms into physical reality, and where desires and intentions take precise form. It is the only level where materiality comes to life—where Light is revealed, allowing us to experience, learn, and transform.

As Divine Light descends from Keter to Malchut, its nature becomes progressively denser, shifting from pure, abstract energy into a tangible manifestation within the world of action. We can observe this transition from the spiritual to the material by looking at how a soccer team operates. The club owner, for example, holds the team's ultimate vision, working primarily in the realm of thought and strategy. The coach, a level below, translates that vision into concrete tactics, crafting game plans and guiding the players. The technical staff, in a more practical and physical role, coordinates training sessions, manages logistics, and ensures every detail supports the team's goals. Finally, the players on the field carry out the most physical effort, bringing the strategy to life during the game.

In soccer, we can appreciate how a goal is not an isolated event, but the culmination of strategies, decisions, passes, and the collective effort of the players on the field. Now, imagine for a moment that we remove the goalposts. What would happen? Without them, the players' efforts lose meaning—there would be no direction, no purpose, no reason to play. Where would they run? What would they defend? Why continue playing? Even if the ball moves across the field and impressive plays unfold, the match would be pointless if there was no possibility of the ball crossing the goal line. The goal gives meaning to every action, transforming each move into a tangible and memorable outcome—just as Malchut grounds the energy of the Sefirot into physical reality.

More than just empty spaces at the field's ends, goalposts establish the clear objective players must achieve. These posts, with their crossbars and nets, delineate the sacred area where goals materialize. In an infinite stadium devoid of goalposts, sideline boundaries, and a set time to score, the drive to act would vanish, and the game would lose its very purpose.

Just as in soccer, where the goal shapes the purpose of the game—directing our actions toward a clear objective—and the goalposts define the space where plays must come to fruition, Malchut represents the final manifestation, channeling energy into matter and giving creation its meaning. Without Malchut, creation would lack purpose, just as a match without goalposts would lose its essence. Through Malchut, we transform challenges into opportunities, as we will explore next, in its paradox where the physical and the spiritual coexist.

The Paradox of Malchut

In Malchut, opposites are integrated and become more evident: Light, which is essentially spiritual and eternal, and matter, which embodies the physical and the temporary. It is in this physical realm that we can achieve the harmonious coexistence of these opposing forces.

This illustrates how every action we take in the physical world entails some form of physical effort. For example, in a soccer match, the grass deteriorates, shoes wear out, and the ball loses elasticity. Even sharing your water with a teammate leaves you with less. This physical reality often feels limited, as resources seem to diminish.

However, while on the physical plane we experience loss, these actions reveal Divine Light, correct aspects of our Tikkun, and foster spiritual growth. What appears to cause wear and tear in the material world is, in fact, becoming a pathway to refine our skills, earn merit, and channel Divine Light, offering a higher perspective on life. Comprehending how the physical and the spiritual intertwine in Malchut allows us to perceive life from a more elevated perspective.

Visualize a lit candle. When it is used to light other candles, its flame neither goes out nor weakens. On the contrary, the light becomes a bridge between the physical and the spiritual, demonstrating its infinite capacity to give without diminishing. The original flame can ignite countless other candles without losing its strength or brightness. For this to happen, the wax must melt—evidence of matter's participation in the process of revealing Light. The wax is the medium that allows the Light to manifest. In this way, we can illuminate an entire room by bringing light, dispelling the darkness.

No matter how dark a room may be, the light within it will continue to shine, because darkness has no power to extinguish the light. A small spark of light is enough to dispel a great amount of darkness, reaffirming the power that light holds over darkness.

A powerful and paradoxical principle in Kabbalah teaches that the greatest spiritual growth arises right after a moment of darkness. It is precisely when we make a mistake or perform a negative action that the greatest opportunity to elevate our consciousness appears. This elevation is possible only if we use that situation as a springboard toward transformation. What initially seems negative thus becomes an opportunity to reveal Light.

Malchut offers us the opportunity to connect with others so that, through these interactions, we may come to know ourselves. We need others to recognize and discover abilities within us that we would otherwise not realize we possess without them. Have you ever thought about the fact that you cannot see your own face directly—that only others can? Seeing your face in a mirror is merely observing a flat, two-dimensional reflection that you interpret as your image. Just as we cannot see our own face without a reflection, we cannot truly understand our essence without the presence of others.

Every interaction we have with another person serves as a mirror. These connections not only reveal our strengths, but also our limitations, challenges, and hidden potential.

By seeing ourselves reflected in others, we can recognize both our light and our shadow.

According to Kabbalah, we cannot correct what we cannot see. It is only through this reflection that we become aware of what needs to be transformed, allowing the light we hide behind our shadows to finally be revealed.

While some traditions suggest that spiritual growth requires distancing ourselves from the material world, Kabbalah teaches that our true work is to transform and elevate the material world we inhabit through physical action. True Tikkun is achieved when we merge the 99% spiritual reality with the 1% physical, allowing the totality of Divine Light to manifest in the material plane where we live.

Malchut reveals the consequences of our actions and our current level of consciousness. Our external reality changes only when we transform our inner being. It is only through a genuine process of internal transformation—through the elevation of our consciousness—that we can truly impact our reality. No matter how tangible it may seem, the reality we perceive is far more flexible than we imagine, for it is intrinsically connected to our level of connection with the Infinite Light and to our ongoing capacity for transformation.

The Desire and the Vessel

In Kabbalah, any desire to receive is symbolized by the

concept of the "vessel," which represents our capacity to receive, contain, and absorb the Divine Light.

In Kabbalah, desire is the precursor to all manifestation. According to this teaching, when desire is pure and aligned with the Light of the Creator, it attracts thoughts, emotions, and actions that allow the Light to materialize. It is through this yearning that Light becomes present in the physical world, taking form in matter.

The purity of our desires influences the thoughts we attract, which in turn trigger our emotions and guide our actions. While we may not always be able to control how we feel, we do have the ability to train our minds to consciously choose thoughts that come from a place of Light and positivity, rather than being driven by automatic or negative thinking.

Just as a flame requires a spark to ignite and a wick to sustain it, Divine Light cannot emerge in this world without a desire to attract it and a Vessel to receive it. The spark is the desire to receive, and the wick is the Vessel, which, when prepared through restraint and the intention to share, allows The Light of the Creator to fully manifest in this physical reality.

A person's vessel is proportional to their level of desire to receive. The greater the desire to receive, the larger the vessel—implying a greater capacity to share Light. However, a stronger desire does not necessarily reflect an altruistic inclination. Some people possess a small vessel because they settle for little in life, which reflects a selfish consciousness, as they seek only to satisfy their personal desires.

Now, what will we fill our Vessels with, and for what purpose? According to Kabbalah, it is essential to fill them with actions that manifest a constant flow of Light, rather than choosing behaviors that offer only immediate gratification. Just like a soccer player, we too must put effort into our daily actions if we want to grow and expand our vessels. The spiritual game is not about settling for less. The Kabbalists teach us that we should aspire to have a large vessel and work with dedication to earn and receive as much Light as possible. In this way, we will have more to share and will sustain the continuous flow of Light.

The Consciousness in Malchut

An action performed in Malchut that sparks a positive transformation—whether in our own life or in the lives of others—generates eternal Light. Such an act not only transforms the individual but also impacts their environment, their children, grandchildren, and future generations. A genuine act of sharing creates an infinite ripple effect, one with the power to generate a profound impact that transcends the physical action itself.

Edson Arantes do Nascimento, known as Pelé, is one of the most iconic players in the history of soccer. Born into a humble family in Brazil, Pelé could not afford to buy a soccer ball. However, his passion was so great that he played in the streets with balls made from socks stuffed with paper. His innate talent did not go unnoticed and caught the eye of Waldemar de Brito, a former soccer player and talent scout, who saw a spark of greatness and decided to support him. De Brito had to persuade Pelé's parents to allow him to take the boy to São Paulo and introduce him to Santos FC, launching his professional career at the age of fifteen.

Waldemar de Brito's act offered Pelé an opportunity not only to transform the young player's life, but also that of his family, his community, and his country. It even changed the history of world soccer, leaving a mark on millions of hearts. Pelé went on to become a soccer legend, winning three World Cups and leaving an indelible legacy in the sport. He inspired generations of players and fans worldwide. A single act can create a lasting impact. We are all channels of Divine Light with the power to make a difference in the lives of others.

The Infinite Light, the Ein Sof, cannot be contained within a Vessel. Therefore, instead of hoarding, we must become pure channels of Light—channels through which the Divine Light flows continuously.

Similarly, at the end of a game, loving parents embrace their child. The hug, though just a limited physical action, cannot possibly contain all the love they feel—there is no number of hugs that could fully express that love. And yet, it is through the physical act of hugging that we are able to channel and express that emotion. Trying to accumulate love instead of giving it makes no sense.

If we observe a hug in isolation, without the consciousness behind it, all we see is a pair of arms wrapped around another person applying pressure. This reflects, once again, that the physical world—without the consciousness that accompanies it—lacks purpose.

Physical objects, on their own, are neither inherently good nor bad. They work as vessels that can either reveal Light or feed our inner voids, depending on the intention behind our actions. For example, one can live happily in a small house with few rooms, just as one could be deeply unhappy in a mansion with many rooms. In a large house, there would simply be more rooms in which to experience unhappiness. A mansion, a luxury car, or the latest smartphone, by themselves, are nothing more than vessels with great potential. Physicality alone cannot fill the void within us. True transformation comes from within; it is not born from external possessions, even though we require the physical world as a tool to reveal Light in our lives. Ultimately, physicality is a means, not the goal.

Concealment and Revelation

Malchut represents revelation—the moment when something becomes defined, finite, and limited. In contrast, Keter symbolizes concealment, where unrevealed potential remains. This is why Kabbalistic writings are written in an enigmatic style, using a language rich in symbolism, archetypes, and stories.

Keeping knowledge concealed preserves its power, just as a seed condenses all its information within a compact and small space. The wisdom we draw from Kabbalistic texts depends on the intensity of our desire, our level of understanding, and the effort we invest. Through the study of Kabbalah, we awaken this concealed knowledge and activate The Light that resides in a "hidden" state.

Our commitment and dedication determine how much we are able to receive and understand this Divine Light.

Kabbalah is not a secret study.

It is the study of secrets.

The Power of Malchut

Throughout this book, we have presented examples from soccer to illustrate how the Sefirot function in this world. However, we can recognize these energies throughout all of creation. Let us now consider an example outside of soccer to demonstrate how the same pattern applies.

A person conceives the idea of creating a film (Keter) and needs to hire a screenwriter (Chochmah) to give it form. The next step would be to engage a production studio capable of evaluating the script and producing and executing the project (Binah). To achieve this, a team is required to carry out the project, corresponding to *Zeir*

Anpin (the grouping of the Sefirot), represented by the sound technicians, cinematographers, lighting specialists, and other essential crew members involved in the making of a film. The actors represent Yesod; they integrate all previous stages by embodying the scenes and bringing the entire creative process into action through each of their performances. Finally, Malchut represents the completed film, ready for us to enjoy.

Malchut is not limited to grand moments of triumph, such as scoring a decisive goal. Every small gesture and daily task are an opportunity to reveal Light in this physical plane. Divinity is not simply present in every place; Divinity constitutes every place, manifesting both in the sublime and in the mundane. Recognizing this allows us to transform every action, no matter how insignificant it may appear, into a means of drawing the Infinite Light of the Creator, elevating us spiritually and reflecting Divine harmony in our reality.

Malchut, far from being a passive state of receiving, is the active process of manifestation. Therefore, Malchut is not merely the endpoint of the Divine Light's manifestation, but the beginning of an eternal cycle. The act of receiving transforms into an expansive act of sharing, generating an infinite ripple that perpetually illuminates and elevates every aspect of our existence. This is the ultimate purpose: to become channels of Light, manifesting the Divine in every aspect of our lives.

Everything we learn through Kabbalah is intended to make us more powerful—not in the sense of dominating or imposing, but in the ability to help others: giving wise advice, healing, building something meaningful, discovering a cure, loving. That is the true meaning of being powerful. Just as a king governs his kingdom, we too can become sovereigns of our own experience, achieving infinite connection by uniting the sovereignty represented by Malchut with the King represented by Keter. The power of a king lies in the ability to forgive and to assist, not in condemning or subjugating.

Malchut is the gateway through which everyone must pass to enter the presence of the King. It is the culmination of all the Sefirot, where Divine Light becomes visible and accessible to the lower world. Just as the earth receives rain from above to produce life, Malchut receives the Divine influx to give life to the lower realms.

(Based on the Zohar's explanation of Malchut)

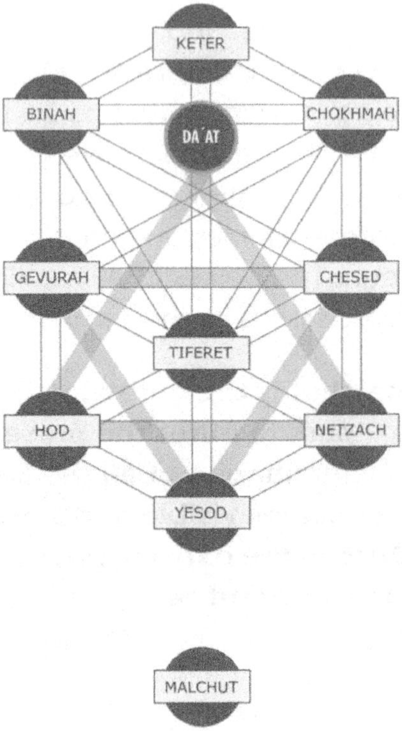

The Star of David represented
in the Tree of Life

THE STAR AND SHIELD OF DAVID

The *Magen David**, also known as the Shield of David or the Star of David, is a symbol rich in profound teachings and mystical meanings. This six-pointed geometric figure emerges from the union of two equilateral triangles: one pointing upward and the other downward, reflecting harmony between opposing and complementary forces.

Each of us carries within the energies of the six Sefirot (*Zeir Anpin*), represented by two triangles. In the human body, these Sefirot are distributed as follows:

First Triangle:

1. **Chesed**: Corresponding to the **right arm.**
2. **Gevurah**: Corresponding to the **left arm.**
3. **Tiferet**: Corresponding to the **torso.**

Second Triangle:

4. **Netzach**: Corresponding to the **right leg.**
5. **Hod**: Corresponding to the **left leg.**
6. **Yesod**: Corresponding to the **genital organs.**

By performing altruistic actions and consciously overcoming our selfish desires, we activate a connection among the Sefirot within our body. This process elevates us from the level of Jacob to the level of Israel. In Kabbalistic terms, this transformation manifests when the lower triangle is superimposed upon the upper triangle, thereby activating the Star of David within ourselves.

This elevation unifies the Tree of Life, allowing the Sefirot to shine as an integrated entity. In this state of unity, our actions—guided by an elevated consciousness of sharing—manifest balanced energies in Malchut (the physical plane), granting us protection and divine revelation. At that moment, the Sefirot are no longer separate entities; they merge and operate as a singular, harmonious force.

The *Magen David* is not merely a star-shaped piece of jewelry worn around the neck; it is a powerful symbol representing the manifestation of Infinite Light in the physical world. When shining in its full splendor, it provides protection and guidance to those who consciously embody it. It stands as a reminder that, by achieving inner balance and acting with altruistic intention, we can transform our reality and connect with the Infinite.

To illustrate this idea through a sports analogy, imagine a soccer team. Each player has a specific role, but the true strength of the team manifests itself when all players work in harmony, united under a shared vision. Similarly, when the Sefirot within us align and act in unity, we elevate our state of existence to a higher level, where every action is imbued with purpose and meaning. Just as a soccer team needs both offense and defense to win, our Sefirot must remain balanced and aligned to manifest the protection and Light of the *Magen David* in our lives.

The *Magen David* becomes a beacon of Light and a shield of protection, igniting the infinite potential within us when we live in harmony with the divine energies. By integrating these teachings into our daily lives, we not only transform our own existence, but also positively impact the world around us.

DAAT

The *Sefer Yetzirah**, or *Book of Formation*, is one of the oldest Kabbalistic texts attributed to the patriarch Abraham. It teaches that there are ten Sefirot—not nine, not eleven, but exactly ten. This specification arises because Daat* is not typically regarded as a Sefirah in its own right. Daat is a complex concept in Kabbalah, and its inclusion as a Sefirah depends on the context in which it is examined.

The Meaning of Daat

Daat translates as "knowledge." Through its acquisition, a profound connection emerges between disparate elements. It represents a state of consciousness where knowledge and experience merge, marking the point where theory transforms into practice and intellectual understanding evolves into lived wisdom.

Daat is also associated with qualities such as memory, concentration, and the vitality of the soul. It is considered a hidden or implicit Sefirah, not always counted in the traditional enumeration of the ten Sefirot of the Tree of

Life. However, it is recognized as a Sefirah that manifests when Keter recedes. Let us explore this further.

The Role of Daat

Imagine a soccer game about to begin: the players step onto the field and assume their positions according to their assigned roles. At this point, the game has not yet started, so the players remain alert but stationary. This lineup mirrors the potential state of the ten Sefirot, from Keter to Malchut, as depicted in the Tree of Life. At this stage, the Sefirot are not yet active, and there is no interaction between them. Consequently, Daat is not formally included in the Tree of Life at this moment. In this phase, there is no revelation of the Divine Light, rendering Daat imperceptible in action.

When the game begins, the sport transitions from a potential to an active state. Keter appears to vanish, but in reality, Keter—embodying the game itself—enables its occurrence. It is like a seed: once it germinates, the seed "disappears" to give rise to the tree that grows. Similarly, Keter recedes once the game commences. At this point, Daat is activated and serves as a bridge facilitating interaction among the players. Thus, at this stage, we can include Daat among the ten Sefirot, as affirmed by the *Sefer Yetzirah*, and it ceases to remain hidden.

On a higher level, Daat functions as the conduit that enables interaction between the upper Sefirot (*Arich Anpin*) and the lower Sefirot (*Zeir Anpin*). Daat is linked to the neck, which connects the head to the body, symbolizing the union between the two.

When our consciousness activates Daat, it facilitates the seamless transmission of knowledge from the most abstract and spiritual levels to the most concrete and manifest. Its purpose is to enable the connection among the Sefirot.

We can compare Daat to the referee (I bet you already thought of this!). The referee possesses complete knowledge of the game's rules, is positioned where the action unfolds, oversees player substitutions, and ensures the game progresses smoothly. They also facilitate communication between events on and off the field and are responsible for upholding the match's continuity. Always present yet unobtrusive, they intervene only when required.

When you examine the representation of the Tree of Life, you see only ten Sefirot listed, and you might conclude that Daat is unnecessary. Similarly, you might think that having a game without a referee is possible. However, in an important match, where the outcome matters, you quickly realize that the referee's role is essential for the game to run smoothly and maintain a fair flow.

Daat: The Bridge of Knowledge and the Activation of Consciousness

Daat is the Sefirah of knowledge and consciousness, acting as a bridge between intellect and emotion and between the finite and the infinite. It is where the Divine Light becomes accessible to human consciousness, enabling unity and harmonization of all the Sefirot. In its elevated state, this connection embodies an altruistic state of being.

In Daat, all the Sefirot exist in their ideal state of infinite sharing, fully revealing the Divine Light. In this state, the distinctions between the Sefirot dissolve, as all radiate infinite Divine Light and operate as a unified whole. This is akin to a soccer team, where interaction and cooperation are crucial for securing victory. If each player aligns with the coach's strategy and acts in harmony, the team operates as a cohesive unit, excelling in defense and unstoppable when scoring goals.

To activate Daat and establish the connection that allows Light to flow through the Sefirot, the practice of *Kavanah* is essential. Translated as "intention," *Kavanah* refers to the direction we give our thoughts when performing any action. It involves focusing the heart and mind on the purpose behind each act, enabling the individual to fully engage with the present moment. *Kavanah* is the mental and emotional element that infuses our actions with meaning and purpose, elevating them beyond mere physical routines.

Practical Example: *Kavanah* in Action

Imagine the following scenario: during a crucial match, a player is distracted. He showers and leaves home on autopilot, drives to the stadium without paying attention to his actions, and hurriedly changes in the locker room, unsure whether he stored his bag in the locker or left the shower running. He forgets to fill his water bottle with cold water, and his entire routine lacks mental presence. Despite his technical skills, his mind is elsewhere, which is reflected in his performance during the game.

In contrast, his teammate prepares with full consciousness. During his shower, he reflects on the tactics he will employ on the field and ensures everything is in order. Before stepping onto the field, he takes a moment to center himself, visualizing the game and his role in it. He is fully present and mindful of every step he takes.

During the match, the distracted player doesn't remember whether he turned off the water in the shower, and his mind jumps from one thought to another. When the critical moment to take penalty shots arrives, whom would you trust with this responsibility?

Both players perform the same physical actions during the game. Both will take three steps and kick the same ball toward the same goalkeeper. However, their *Kavanah* is vastly different. The distracted player's lack of presence and concentration reduces his actions into mere mechanical movements, diminishing his chances of success. His legs may be on the field, but the rest of his being is absent.

In summary, Daat is pivotal within the Kabbalistic structure of the Tree of Life. It connects and activates the Sefirot, enabling the revelation of the Divine Light on the physical plane. The practice of *Kavanah* is crucial for activating this connection, elevating our actions, and allowing the Divine Light to manifest in all aspects of our lives. Just as a referee is essential for a fluid and fair soccer game, Daat is vital for the harmony and flow of the Sefirot, guiding us toward a higher elevated conscious existence.

ADDED TIME, OVERTIME AND LUCK

Added time consists of the additional minutes added by the referee to compensate for interruptions during the match. There is also overtime, an additional period played when a match ends in a draw to determine the winner. In tournaments like the World Cup, approximately 25%[3] of games are decided during added time, extra time, or penalty shootouts.

1

[3] This figure includes an estimate of goals scored during stoppage time at the end of each half, as well as goals scored during extra time and penalty shootouts, based on data from the last three World Cups.

These minutes are filled with intense tension as time runs out to score the goals needed to secure victory. Everything that was not achieved in the ninety minutes of regular play can be decided in these final moments.

As this resource becomes scarcer, we feel the urgency to act and make the most of every instant. By understanding its value, we recognize that each minute carries a unique opportunity. This pressure compels us to focus on what truly matters and to maximize our chances. Appreciating the gift of time leads us to deeply value this irreplaceable resource, whose scarcity is one of the most powerful catalysts for action.

"If it weren't for the last minute,
nothing would get done"
Murphy's Law

Time grants us multiple chances to achieve our goals and offers opportunities to rectify our actions. However, it is a resource we must not squander.

In Kabbalah, situations are never random events. Life unfolds as it should, in harmony and balance, governed by perfectly synchronized laws of cause and effect. Everything that happens to you is orchestrated FOR YOU. It is the Creator's ultimate act of kindness: offering you the opportunity to undergo this experience and attain merit through the lessons you need at every moment.

Thus, the moment your life unfolds is called the "present" because, in essence, it is a gift.

Life is always working in your favor. Often, we are unaware of this, just as we fail to appreciate the events that don't occur—like the problems we never encounter. Most of the time, we simply move forward without acknowledging the challenges from which we have been spared. However, when you can clearly perceive a situation where life has whistled in your favor, we call that "luck."

In Hebrew, *luck* is *Mazal**, an acronym for three words:

M*akom* translates as **place.**

Z'man translates as **time.**

L*imud* translates as **knowledge**, or *La'asot*, which means **to act.**

"Luck," therefore, means deserving to be in the right place at the right time, with the knowledge and capacity to act... and the awareness to recognize how life plays in your favor.

WHAT GAME DO YOU CHOOSE TO WATCH?

Every soccer fan knows that surprises can happen until the very last second and that the game is not over until the referee blows the final whistle. In a match, as in your life, every passing second represents 100% of your life unfolding. There is not a single moment when the game isn't happening at its full potential, offering everything you need in that instant to experience what you're meant to. Right now (regardless of when you're reading this), your game continues as the clock ticks on—whether you are making the most of it or letting it slip away.

Judging the situation you find yourself in at any given moment is like tasting a fruit before it has ripened; you might think it's bitter and inedible when, in reality, it hasn't completed its maturation process. Similarly, your life is constantly evolving—it's still unfolding.

Have you ever watched a soccer game and noticed the difference between what's happening on the field and how your mind idealizes each play? It's as if two versions of the same game are taking place: one in reality and another that exists only in your mind, where you judge and reinterpret every move you see. This duality is why we feel frustrated during a sports match; we're not truly appreciating the game being played but rather the one we imagine and mistake for reality. Observing the actual game on the field and the one playing out in our minds are entirely different experiences.

It's the same with our lives. Sometimes, events don't align with our expectations about how life "should" be happening. Instead of embracing what is truly happening, we start judging the situations. This leads us to create a mental narrative that deviates from reality, creating a parallel world that exists only in our minds. This prevents us from fully living the life unfolding before us and from effectively addressing our challenges.

You can experience the game as it is, or you can dwell on how it should unfold to be "better" according to your opinion. As if soccer needed your opinion to be better. The game unfolds regardless, while you waste your time thinking about how it should unfold.

In every situation in your life, just as in the next game you watch, ask yourself: **What game do you choose to watch?**

THE CONSCIOUS GAME

When a thought arises, who is having that thought? A thought does not think itself; there is a consciousness that sustains it. That consciousness is your essence, which must inhabit a physical body in this world to experience being a conscious player.

The process of awakening begins with a first step: realizing that you are asleep. This moment of awareness brings you into the present—into the game of your life—where you can appreciate every situation. Every passing moment is worth living to the fullest, because you have never lived that moment before, and it will not come again. Every step, every play on the field carries deep meaning and is filled with opportunity. Your life offers you the chance to awaken at any moment, because it is being created in every instant.

The time has come to step onto the field, but this time, consciously. Being a conscious player means learning to perceive the game as it truly free from selfish desires, expectations, or unmanaged emotions. From now on, you'll realize that although the game, the stadium, the opposing team, the field, the ball, and even you remain the same, this time, you can now experience the field in a completely different way. What changed? You now have the tools to live consciously.

Here are some fundamental ideas of what being a conscious player means to me:

- We must understand that the Divine Light is more powerful than darkness; the latter is merely an illusion.

- We have been playing the game of life without understanding its rules, and we have been playing on the wrong field, seeking achievements in the 1% physical world of effects.

- The true playing field is within us, where the most important battles take place.

- All our senses are directed outward, but it is we who are the ones experiencing everything internally; in truth, everything happens within us.

- An external event cannot dictate how we should interpret it. No event has meaning outside of us.

Only through our interpretation do we give meaning to what we experience.

- Running away from your life and avoiding what you are meant to face makes no sense. For if you run away, where else can you go? You'll end up meddling in other people's lives.

- We think that external events or people are the cause of our suffering or joy. But these situations are merely reflections. Circumstances arise so we can recognize something we wouldn't otherwise see—something that would remain hidden from us without this reflection.

- We are responsible for our lives; accepting this empowers us to make choices. If we don't, we remain slaves to our desires and, consequently, the emotions they generate within us.

- Receiving advice and learning from others is essential for growing along our path. However, as tempting as it may be to follow instructions blindly, doing so hands over your free will to another, hindering your progress in your game. We came into this world to exercise our free will, not to live as the shadow of others.

- You are in a game where the opposing team will try to keep you busy and distracted at every turn. It wants you to believe that the game's objective is to satisfy your desire to receive for yourself alone and that external events, things, and people are the means to fill these selfish desires. But the true purpose of the game is to use your skill to dribble past distractions and lift the veils that prevent you from being a channel of Infinite Light in this world, thus attaining the fulfillment you long for.

- Kabbalah teaches us that others make miracles possible in our lives, just as we are miracles for others. We must dedicate ourselves to positively influence our surroundings.

- While one must be aware of the Creator to connect with Him, it is not necessary to be aware of the *Yetzer Hara* to constantly serve it and be controlled by it.

- Your mind dislikes paradoxes because they make no sense to it. Yet, paradoxes are gateways to higher levels of knowledge. Embracing the paradox and realizing that, in fact, it makes sense is key to expanding our consciousness and understanding.

- The paradox lies in that, to receive all The Light, we must not seek it out. Instead, we must share it and act as The Light itself does. In the process, we learn to transform our desire to receive for ourselves into a desire to influence and share with others.

- The game has its predetermined rules, its beginning and its end. Within that timeframe, we have the free will to play as we choose. The game has no preference for how you play or where you take the ball. The game will support you unconditionally wherever you choose to go.

- In soccer, the fleeting glory goes to the one who scores the goal, but the coach records every move: who made the assists to score, who knows how to play as a team, and who was truly valuable on the field. That record remains for when you negotiate your promotion as a player. Similarly, a cosmic record documents not only our victories and challenges but also all the moves and passes we make or fail to make. Every desire, thought, emotion, choice, and action leave an imprint in the 99% spiritual world. Nothing that happens in your life is in vain.

- During soccer training, the way you talk to your brain can significantly influence your performance. If you give negative instructions, such as "run to the end of the course, but don't hit any orange cones," your brain has to constantly spot those cones and keep in mind that hitting them is forbidden. This creates a constant sense of threat, distracting you from your goal—which is to reach the target instead of focusing on the obstacles in your path. On the other hand, positive instructions like "reach the end of the field by following the marked path" allows your brain to focus on the goal rather than the distractions of what not to do. Training to think positively has a special power that facilitates smoother and more effective progress toward your goals.

- The power of giving yourself positive instructions lies in directing your attention toward your goal rather than feeding distractions.

- You may think you lack self-confidence, but in reality, it simply means you've decided to accept that belief. If you can choose to believe that you don't trust yourself, why not choose to embrace the possibility that you do? In the end, both are simply suggestions from your mind, and you have the power to decide which to choose.

- We have gotten it backward. We place our certainty in our doubts, yet we doubt that things could turn out well.

- If you pause for a moment to ask your life what it's doing with you right now, it will answer that it's giving you the fullest life it has to offer. It doesn't know how to do anything but give you everything you need in each moment. In return, it asks nothing more than for you to live it.

Consider a universal example beyond soccer to illustrate how our mind works: Some children believe there are monsters in their closet, and that belief terrifies them. They vividly imagine these creatures, giving them personalities, even though they have never seen them nor heard of anyone being devoured by such beings. The monster exists as long as we feed it.

The Kabbalist Yehuda Ashlag explains:

"A person changes when the pain of staying in a situation becomes greater than the pain of changing."

It is then, with great fear and effort, that the child decides to approach the closet—trembling in the darkness of the room. With eyes barely open, he musters the courage to open it and face whatever awaits inside, only to discover that it's empty. In that instant, the monster loses its power and disappears, because it is no longer needed. The only power the monster has is the one we give it by believing it's real.

When we grow up, we still fear the monsters in the closet, but now they're "serious" adult concerns. Yet the way to face them remains the same: walk to the closet, open it, and look inside.

Some people think, "How nerve-wracking! It's exhausting! I'd rather sleep with the door open, a dim hallway light on, and my phone glowing, numbing what I feel because it's too intense." That's a valid choice, but each moment offers you an opportunity—one you can choose to embrace or reject.

FNAL WRDS

You may have read FINAL WORDS, but that is not what the title says. Let us remember that our brain needs things to make sense, not necessarily to be true. Let us take a moment to recap, and you will see how we have already learned to read between the lines.

In my search for a definition of the game of soccer I found the following explanation from an AI: “The objective of the game is to move a ball across the field and attempt to place it into the opponent’s net, an action known as scoring a goal. The team that scores the most goals by the end of the match is the winner.” In short, as I understand it, the objective seems to be WINNING, a purpose achieved by scoring more goals than the opposing team.

While one might argue that playing soccer encompasses more than just winning—such as enjoying the sport, bonding with friends, staying fit, or feeling the adrenaline rush—the rationale behind every play is rooted in the primary goal: winning. If you consult the rules of any sport or board game, the objective is always to win, to come first, to surpass others. You won't find a coach advising the team to focus on enjoying the game in the final minutes of a tied championship match. Nor will there be substitutions to ensure every player gets equal time, because the purpose of the game is to win. Every decision is focused on achieving that goal.

If it's evident that the objective is to win, why don't we often play against small children, against whom we could easily score countless goals effortlessly, thus achieving victory without complications, fulfilling the objective?

Consider this scenario: if someone offered you a special power that guaranteed victory in every championship you entered, with an overwhelming goal difference in your favor, would it make sense to accept? It might seem tempting at first, but you would soon realize you are trapped in the most boring game imaginable, devoid of emotion or meaning. You would find yourself in an empty, purposeless state.

Imagine another situation: your father attends all your soccer games throughout the season. Time and again, you score the winning goal, and your team always emerges victorious. Each time you score, you look to your father, seeing his pride in your achievements. Then you discover that he paid for you to score those goals and that all the team's victories were prearranged. How would you feel?

Let's pause to reflect: If the objective was not winning and the true purpose was having fun, why do we get frustrated when we lose, miss a penalty, suffer a foul, or when the referee fails to call a play in our favor?

The problem with the previous scenarios is that winning lacks genuine merit. To achieve true merit, the possibility of losing must exist. Kabbalists teach that, in simple terms, we ask for a challenge to obtain all the satisfaction that comes from winning. Being deserving is what brings true fulfillment. The risk of losing is what gives meaning to the concept of victory. It is our choice to come to this physical world to work, earn, and win the infinite satisfaction that comes from transforming our nature.

The ten Sefirot were created to gradually tame the Divine Light. When The Light reaches the physical world of Malchut, its emanation is hidden from our perception. This offers us the opportunity to carry out our spiritual work in an environment where we can use free will to earn and reveal our divine nature. Only through effort and challenging situations can we fully savor and appreciate satisfaction.

There is a fundamental difference between the game of soccer and the game of life. As we have established, the objective in soccer is to win—to defeat the opposing team.

In the game of life, in this game that is YOUR LIFE, the goal is also to win—but not against an external opponent, not against another team or anything outside yourself. The true objective is to identify your *Yetzer Hara* in every moment, uncover what it reveals to you, confront it, and dismantle the barrier that separates you from Divine Light.

The paradox of life is to live both realities simultaneously. You step onto the field to play against another team, giving it your all, while at the same time knowing that, in truth, there is no other team. When we step onto the field, we are immersed in the game of recognizing ourselves through the reflection of others. The opposing team acts as a mirror, revealing our strengths and weaknesses, our deepest fears and aspirations. Competing against and outscoring becomes a necessary excuse to give the game meaning, a way to test ourselves through interaction with other players. We come to appreciate a player's greatness when they face an opponent of equal caliber in situations that challenge them to give their best.

Thus, the experience on the field becomes our wisest teacher. In the game of life, we all win. There are no mistakes or failures, only decisions that consciously or unconsciously lead us to the next play. You may reach the championship's pinnacle or need to return to the field repeatedly to keep progressing. Sometimes you win, but you always learn!

If you have reached the end but don't feel at peace or illuminated, it simply means you haven't reached the end yet.

WHEN THE STUDENT AWAKENS,
THE TEACHER DISAPPEARS...

LET'S PLAY

I'd like to close with a few questions. After reading this book, you now have the tools to arrive at the answers yourself. Surely, your approach to these questions is quite different now compared to before reading this book.

Here we go...

What game are we playing?

When did the game begin?

Where is this game being played?

What does the soccer field represent?

What does the game represent?

What does the ball represent?

What is the objective of the game?

How can we receive this Light?

Who is the opposing team?

Who are the players that make up the *Yetzer Hara's* team?

Okay, but how do I fulfill my role on the field?

How long does the game last?

What happens if the other team scores on me?

What happens if, while learning, I make mistakes on the field?

There are many rules—are there any I should always keep in mind?

The answers to these questions, along with the opportunity to contact me and leave a review of this book, can be found here.

www.meiler.com/soccer

GLOSSARY

Abraham: The first patriarch, known for his faith and covenant with God. He is associated with the Sefirah of Chesed (mercy).

Abraham Azulai (1570–1643): A Sephardic rabbi and Kabbalist of the 17th century, author of works such as *Chesed L'Avraham* and *Or HaChama*.

Aharon: Brother of Moses and the first high priest. He is associated with the Sefirah of **Hod** (glory).

Arich Anpin: "Long Face," representing an elevated aspect of divinity from the upper Sefirot of Keter, Chochmah, and Binah.

Baal HaSulam (1885–1954): Meaning "The Master of the Ladder" in Hebrew, this is the honorary title given to Rav Yehuda Ashlag for his extensive commentary and translation of the *Zohar*, known as *HaSulam* (*The Ladder*).

Bar Mitzvah: Marks the moment when a young man reaches the age of thirteen and assumes religious and communal responsibilities as an adult within the Jewish tradition.

Bereshit: The first word of the Torah, meaning "In the beginning." It is also the name of the Torah's first book (*Genesis*), which narrates the creation of the world.

Binah (understanding): The third Sefirah, representing the process of expanding and comprehending wisdom.

Daat (knowledge): is not an independent Sefirah. It is the deep inner consciousness that enables the practical application of knowledge and acts as a bridge between the Sefirot.

David: King of Israel, known for defeating Goliath. He is associated with the Sefirah of **Malchut**.

Ein Sof (Endless): The infinite essence of God, beyond any definition or limitation.

Esau: Son of Isaac and twin brother of Jacob, known for selling his birthright.

Gevurah (judgment): The fifth Sefirah, representing judgment, restraint, and discipline. It is the force that establishes boundaries and complements the expansiveness of Chesed.

HaSulam: Meaning "The Ladder" in Hebrew, the name given to Rav Yehuda Ashlag's extensive commentary and translation of the *Zohar*. This monumental work was completed between 1943 and 1953 and aims to make the *Zohar* more accessible and comprehensible for Kabbalah students.

Hod (glory): The eighth Sefirah, symbolizing humility, gratitude, and reverence. Hod is the ability to surrender and give thanks, complementing the victory of Netzach.

Isaac: The second patriarch, son of Abraham and father of Jacob. He is associated with the Sefirah of **Gevurah** (judgment).

Isaac Luria (1534–1572): A 16th-century rabbi and mystic known as the Ari or Arizal, whose teachings transformed Kabbalah.

Jacob: Son of Isaac, the third patriarch, also known as Israel. He had twelve sons who formed the tribes of Israel. He is associated with the Sefirah of **Tiferet** (beauty)

Chesed (mercy): The fourth Sefirah, associated with mercy, kindness, and unconditional love. It represents abundance and the generosity of giving without limits.

Chochmah (wisdom): The second Sefirah, symbolizing divine wisdom and the first point of creation from Keter. It represents the initial spark of inspiration and pure knowledge.

Kabbalah: A Jewish mystical tradition that seeks to understand the divine nature and the universe. It explains the mystical aspect and purpose of the Torah.

Kavanah: Meaning "intention" or "direction." It refers to the focus and intentionality in a prayer, study, and other spiritual acts.

Keter (crown): The first and highest of the Sefirot, representing Divine Will and the purpose of creation. It is the source of all blessings and the root of all desires.

Kippah: A small round cap worn by observant Jews as a sign of respect and reverence toward God.

Klipa (plural: Klipot): "Shell" or "husk" that obscures Divine Light, associated with negative forces.

Magen David: Known as the Shield of David or Star of David, it consists of two interlaced triangles forming a six-pointed star. In Jewish mysticism, it is associated with spiritual protection and the six Sefirot of Malchut.

Malchut (kingdom): The tenth and final Sefirah, representing manifestation and receptivity. Malchut is the realm of realization and the ultimate expression of all previous influences, symbolizing divine presence in the material world.

Mazal: Hebrew word for "luck," representing *makom* (*place*), *z'man* (*time*), and *limmud* (*knowledge*). It signifies that being in the right place at the right time, with the right understanding, creates our own luck.

Mitzvah (plural: Mitzvot): The 613 commandments or ordinances in Judaism, designed to help us connect and unite with the Creator through their observance.

Moses Cordovero (1522–1570): Also known as the Ramak, a 16th-century rabbi and Kabbalist, author of *Pardes Rimonim*.

Moses de Leon (1240–1305): A 13th-century rabbi and Jewish mystic. Tradition holds that he compiled the *Zohar* from teachings orally transmitted since the time of Rabbi Shimon Bar Yochai.

Nachshon ben Aminadav: Leader of the tribe of Judah, known for his faith in crossing the Red Sea.

Netzach (eternity): The seventh Sefirah, representing persistence, victory, and perpetuity. It is the energy of continuity and resilience.

Or Choser: "Returning Light" in Hebrew, referring to Light that is not passively received but is reflected or returned to its source. It represents the ability to receive and transmit Divine Light through our actions in the physical world.

Or Yashar: "Direct Light" in Hebrew, referring to Divine Light flowing directly and unhindered, filling vessels according to their desire.

Rabbi Shimon Bar Yochai (approx. 100–160 CE): A Jewish sage and mystic of the 2nd century, considered the principal author of the *Zohar*.

Rah: Translated from Hebrew as "evil."

Ratzon Atzmi: A Hebrew term referring to the selfish desire to receive for oneself without intention to share.

Ratzon Lehashpia: A Hebrew term referring to the altruistic desire to give and share with others.

Satan: "Adversary" in Hebrew, representing the inclination toward selfishness. It is the name given in the *Zohar* to the angel who fought with Jacob.

Sefer Yetzirah: *Book of Formation*, a foundational Kabbalistic text exploring the creation of the universe. Tradition attributes its authorship to the patriarch Abraham.

Sefirah (plural: Sefirot): Ten attributes or emanations through which divine energy manifests and interacts with the world. Each Sefirah is a specific emanation of these ten.

Shema Israel: A central declaration of faith in Judaism affirming God's oneness with the words, "Hear, O Israel: the Lord is our God, the Lord is One." In Kabbalah, it symbolizes the unity between the individual and the divine.

Talmud Eser Sefirot: A Kabbalistic work by Rav Yehuda Ashlag that explores the ten Sefirot and their interactions.

Tefillin: Small leather boxes containing parchment scrolls with biblical texts, worn during morning prayers.

Tikkun: "Correction" or "repair," a process of restoring harmony in the universe and in an individual's life.

Tiferet (beauty): The sixth Sefirah, representing harmony and beauty. It is the balanced combination of Chesed and Gevurah.

Torah: The Hebrew Bible, comprising the five books of Moses.

Yehuda Ashlag (1885–1954): Kabbalist known as Baal HaSulam, who translated and commented on the *Zohar*. His work, *HaSulam* (*The Ladder*), includes and extensive commentary to make the *Zohar* more accessible to students of Kabbalah.

Yetzer Hara: The inclination toward evil or negative impulses within us that can lead to selfish or destructive actions.

Yesod (foundation): The ninth Sefirah, acting as the channel of communication and connection between the higher Sefirot and Malchut. It represents the base of all emanations and the force of union and transmission.

Yosef (Joseph): Son of Jacob. Sold by his brothers, he became a leader in Egypt. He is associated with the Sefirah of **Yesod** (foundation).

Zeir Anpin: "Small Face," a set of six Sefirot: Chesed, Gevurah, Tiferet, Netzach, Hod, and Yesod, aspects of divinity manifested in the physical world.

Zohar: Meaning 'Splendor' in Hebrew, it is the principal text of Kabbalah. Attributed to the sage Rabbi Shimon Bar Yochai, it is written in Aramaic and comprises a collection of mystical commentaries on the Torah, revealing hidden meanings in the scriptures. It addresses themes such as the nature of God, the soul, and the purpose of creation. It is regarded as a key to unlocking the universe's deepest secret.

ABOUT THE AUTHOR

Neron Meiler is a pioneer in digital innovation and consciousness expansion, with over two decades leading one of Miami's top digital marketing agencies. His work bridges creativity, technology, and neuroscience—reshaping the modern marketing landscape.

Beyond business, Neron has spent over 26 years immersed in Kabbalah, the ancient wisdom that offers practical tools for living with awareness and purpose. He has contributed to global platforms like *Dailyzohar.com* and co-created mobile apps such as *TZADIKIM* and *UNITY ZOHAR*, making spiritual teachings accessible through digital tools.

Kabbalah and Soccer—his first book—is the product of six years of deep reflection. Using soccer as a metaphor, he explores how the Tree of Life and the Sefirot can guide us in navigating life's challenges. His mission is to help readers connect with their true potential and play the game of life with clarity, intention, and heart.

Made in United States
Orlando, FL
12 September 2025

64920659R00105